THEOLOGY
FOR
DUMMIES

THEOLOGY FOR DUMMIES

CHUCK CORWIN with C.V. MATHEW

ISPCK & UBS
2008

Theology for Dummies – Published by the Rev. Dr. Ashish Amos of the Indian Society for Promoting Christian Knowledge (ISPCK), Post Box 1585, Kashmere Gate, Delhi-110006 with UBS (Union Biblical Seminary), Post Box 1425, Bibvewade, Pune-411037, Maharashtra.

© Author, 2006

Revised Edition, 2008

All rights reserved. No part of this book may be reproduced or transmitted in any form or by any means, electronic, mechanical, photocopying, recording, or by any information storage and retrieval system, without the prior permission in writing from the publisher.

The views of this book are those of the authors and the publisher takes no responsibility for any of the statements.

ISBN: 978-81-8458-061-7

Laser typeset by **ISPCK,** Post Box 1585, 1654, Madarsa Road, Kashmere Gate, Delhi-110006
Tel: 23866323/22
e-mail: ashish@ispck.org.in • ella@ispck.org.in
website: www.ispck.org.in

CONTENTS

Dedication vii
Why This Book? ix

THEOLOGY: TOOL FOR FAITH

1. Why Study Theology? 3
2. Disclosure 7
3. Helps 13
4. Sharpeners 19
5. Awareness 23
6. Approaches 27
7. Say That Again 35

THE FATHER

8. The Almighty 45
9. Looking 49
10. Proofs 51
11. Denial 54
12. Creation and Providence 56
13. Grace 62

THE SON

14. Incarnation 67
15. The Cross 71
16. Resurrection 75
17. Christology 78

MAN

18. Christian Anthropology 83
19. Postmodernism 92
20. Evil 94
21. Pilgrimage I 99
22. Pilgrimage II 105

THE HOLY SPIRIT

23. The Re-Creator 115
24. The Church 120
25. The Trans-Creator 127
26. Music 132
27. Worship 136
28. Ministry 138

Index 142

TO CHACKO CHACKO
friend and overseer
of
books, students, staff, faculty
brothers and sisters of the common life
at
Union Biblical Seminary

WHY THIS BOOK?

It takes one to know one. This book is written by a dummy who didn't clearly define terms like *faith, grace, or salvation* before using them. In Japan, audiences dutifully listened to my translations of the above terms. Those translations jarred the Japanese mind; there was an aura of foreignness about them that made a person less Japanese if accepted at face value. I used nouns; they used verbs. Frustrated, I immersed myself in Japanese idiom, searching for new expressions to replace old ones. Eternal truth clothed in new garments made the message come alive. Japanese hearers responded. Surprisingly, their newfound faith poured life into obsolete words and baptized new ones for contemporary use. But one cannot break away from traditional expressions unless truth behind them is properly understood.

In India I experienced the same frustration. For a different reason. At English-medium Union Biblical Seminary I was set free from the laborious task of finding equivalents in the Indian vernacular.

However, to my chagrin, I discovered students were using English theological words as mantras, plugging them in papers here and there, mere jargon that confused the meaning. For them and those like them this is written. With the reader I go back to basics, going over words and phrases that appear in theological discourse, giving Greek origins, defining them, and finally showing their significance for the Christian life. If the answer is not self-evident, I will ask the question Luther posed in one of his sermons, "Christ is not called Christ because he has two natures. *What is that to me?*"

My chief reference is *The Westminster Dictionary of Christian Theology,* 1983 edition. Names of authors quoted will follow the reference, but thereafter only quotation marks are used until the next author is quoted. Proper referencing of other texts is given at the bottom of each page. Most vignettes come from a companion volume, *Return to Chaos*. Helpful criticism by Dr. K.V. Abraham of Union Biblical Seminary is much appreciated.

THEOLOGY – TOOL FOR CLARIFYING FAITH

1. Why study theology?

If I remember correctly, he belonged to the Tendai sect of Japanese Buddhism. Dressed in brown kimono and dark blue shawl, the priest with shaved head stood behind a small podium. His task was to explain Eastern understanding of the universe. From his lips poured out words that baffled our Western minds: "Everything is emptiness. All is continually changing." I had learned in seminary the peril of all-ness statements, so thought I would have a little fun.

"Sir, would you mind writing that last statement on the blackboard?"

He wrote in large Japanese characters, "All is continually changing."

"Is that statement included in the 'All'?"

"Of course."

"Then the proposition 'all is continually changing' could someday mean 'some things never change'."

"You are imposing Western logic on Eastern thought," he answered, visibly irritated.

The above exchange elicited rudeness from me and anger from the priest, never the intent of theological discourse. Knowledge of God and his ways should draw us closer to him and closer to others. We have friends uninformed about Christian faith, its truths and values. We want to share our beliefs with them but haven't sorted out ancient and orthodox doctrines or modern variations thereof. Even supposing a book like this could help, the greatest hurdle has yet to be cleared. Few ask questions we are prepared to answer. How to begin? Why not as Jesus did, by getting involved with people at their point of need? Ask questions about their personal situation. Be a careful listener. Probe deeper. Theological learning does not take place in a vacuum. With that in mind, I begin each major section with a vignette like the one above.

Jesus did not explain God in a classroom but as he and his disciples encountered life situations. When they followed him along the roads of Palestine, among the Judean hills, and during lake crossings, Jesus stressed they would recognize truth about God through obedience. Jesus' practical approach to theology reminds Christians in every age to translate theological knowledge into daily living. As lives of great saints attest, obedience to truth, not full apprehension of it, is God's appointed way for learning more about him.

Theology - Tool for Clarifying Faith

Theologies appeared soon after the church was born. Terse outlines of Christian faith — the Apostles Creed, the Nicene Creed, the Athanasian Creed — provided the early church a worshipful response to scripture, a standard in times of persecution, a guide for theological study, and a defense against heresy.

M. Erickson gives several reasons we should study theology today: (1) *correct doctrinal beliefs* are necessary for establishing a relationship between us and the Father; (2) *truth determines our actions:* "All human experience implies the element of thought. Man must think even if he is the most primitive devotional Christian."[1] And if thought determines our actions, correct theology is crucial for right action; (3) *ideological alternatives face us today* — humanism, secularism, materialism and postmodernism.

Isn't the Bible enough? Yes, until I explain it in my own words. It is then that I create a "theology." The word comes from two Greek words, *theos* and *logos*, which mean *God* and *reason*. Theology is the discipline of reasoning about God. However, there is a problem. Since finite minds can never comprehend the infinite, theology is an imprecise science. To know fully is to dominate. If our minds could completely comprehend God, he would

---

[1] Paul Tillich, *A History of Christian Thought,* Harper and Row, 1968, p.xi.

become an object of our reflection; we would be God. No. His ways are past finding out. He is the subject, we are the object. There is another reason why theology is imprecise. Studying God implies studying his works—creation, providence, and salvation. Though God himself "changes not," our perceptions of him do as he works in history to accomplish his purpose. Theology, therefore, is not a fixed body of knowledge; rather, it is a tool for clarifying faith.

Erickson defines theology as "the discipline which strives to give a coherent statement of the doctrines of the Christian faith, based primarily upon Scripture, placed in the context of culture, worded in contemporary idiom, and related to issues of life."[2] This last point—related to issues of life—is crucial for future laymen emerging from college campuses. Their interest in theology is not academic but practical. When asked about the meaning of life, springs of peace and joy, motivation for integrity, criterion for right and wrong, tolerance in the face of bigotry, hope in the midst of tragedy, they should be able to provide answers derived from Christian faith.

Theology lives when it gives meaningful answers to questions arising out of the human situation. We will ask questions asked throughout church history,

---

[2] M. Erickson, *Christian Theology* I, Grand Rapids: Baker Book House, 1983, p.21.

mention theological answers given, then point out which seem to agree with Scripture and fit the present historical context. We may not agree with a scholar's treatment of a particular subject, nor with his conclusions. But we cannot fully grasp, appreciate or defend our own position until we consider its alternatives. Hearing other views enriches our own; we may even gain fresh insights that do more justice to scripture than do ours.

There are two main doctrines in the Bible — God created the world and sent his Son to redeem it. All other doctrines arose in their defense: prophets thundered against idolatry, Jesus countered pharisaism, Paul struggled with legalism, John warned about incipient gnosticism. Lessons from Asian church history demonstrate that non-theological Christianity cannot survive. For example, from the seventh to the twelfth centuries Nestorian missionaries to China presented an incarnate Christ with two distinct persons: one human, one divine. Confused Chinese converts were later swept away by Islam.

2. Disclosure

What does Revelation mean? — To reveal means literally, *to unveil.* The Greek word, *apokalupsis,* from which it is derived, meant the disclosure of something previously unknown. When used in theology it refers to God's action in making truth known to man, truth about his character or purposes which would not occur to us. God normally reveals himself through conscience, creation, history, scripture, and occasionally by spectacular dreams or flashes of inner vision.

Since Thomas Aquinas (13th century) theologians have distinguished between *natural theology* — truths about God which are self-evident in nature, and *revealed theology* — truths about God which cannot be apprehended by human reason alone, such as God's justifying the ungodly, the Trinity, etc. Until modern times, most people believed God revealed himself through the prophets and apostles, and what they heard was written down as scripture.

With the advent of *higher criticism* of the Bible by 19th century German scholars, some theologians shifted from finding revelation in scripture to the *events* scripture tells and to the *faith* which grasps them. Revelation, they say, occurs when a person in faith believes the mystery of the incarnation, not when a person reads the manger story in Matthew for the first time. However, this reduces the validity of God's revelation not to his accomplished acts in history nor their record but to man's subjective apprehension of them.

Can human language express God's revelation? — Whenever we talk about God, we use words and expressions that have emerged from culture. But how can finite beings speak intelligently about an infinite God? Answers to this perplexing question are varied. On the positive side, classical Christian theology "presupposes that we are able to speak of God, since God has created us with reason by virtue of which we share in the divine mind" (Donovan). Aquinas believed that we can use human terms for explaining God by *analogy* because of the relation between creature and Creator; Barth parried, saying only the gift of faith makes theological knowledge possible. However, most Protestant theologians justify the use of human language because God did so in revealing himself to prophets and apostles.

As if schooled in Brahmanism (a term that covers orthodox Hinduism and the caste system,) some Western thinkers explain God in negative terms — not this, not that (*neti, neti* in Sanskrit). For example, Rudolph Otto believed religious awareness cannot be described in human terms and coined the term *wholly other*. His was a bold attempt to exempt theological knowledge from the scientific method which limits truth to observable data. Otto needed not to worry; a quantifiable approach to all knowledge falls prey to its own methodology. The theory itself is not verifiable by the scientific method.

What is a symbol? The vocabulary and grammar of a particular language, both in its spoken and written forms, constitute a *symbol system*. The word symbol came from the Greek *sumballos*, which was coined from two Greek words, *sum* (with) and *ballos* (throw), and means literally *to throw together*. Any word or object becomes a symbol when culture invests it with sufficient emotive power to transport the user beyond the word or object to the reality expressed. For example, bread and wine in Communion are symbols of Christ's body and blood. Christian culture has invested bread and wine with sufficient emotive power to transport the communicant beyond those elements to the body and blood of Christ. For our study we will use the word *symbol* in this rich, emotional sense.

Any language or symbol system has imbedded within it the cosmology or religious philosophy of the people using it. For example, the Chinese symbol system is one of ideographs, containing component parts of the human body, so that a humanistic philosophy is imparted to Chinese people from childhood. In summary, a symbol system represents the world but also becomes the means for understanding it. Thus, in India with over 26 major language groups, perceptions of the world vary from state to state, individual to individual.

Others have stressed that the full meaning of a religious language can only be understood by native speakers. As people develop a religious tradition, word-meaning is shaped by common experience.

Religious language, then, enables people to live out beliefs, but faith pours back into those words dynamic meaning. Religious language and faith are interdependent.

When we use symbols about God, we realize that no symbol conveys his essence; that is wholly unknown to us. On the other hand, we see the effects of God's creation and providence. We speak of God's beauty, his power, his creativity. These symbols originally found their meaning in the created world. "All things share, in graded proportion (Greek *analogeia*), in this outpouring of being" (Williams). God wills to share his life; hence, we can learn about him through his manifestations. Church liturgy and art mediate the knowledge of God. But they are partial. A religious symbol uses the mundane of ordinary experience in speaking of God, but in such a way that the ordinary meaning of the material used is both affirmed and denied. Every religious symbol affirms and negates itself in the literal sense. God is a Rock, but isn't a rock; God is a Strong Tower, but not a tower.

Lives of the saints—OT patriarchs and NT saints—demonstrate what it is like to be shaped by symbols of religious faith. "Each believing or faith-directed life is therefore a potential symbol for talking about God." This is why we preach from the lives of Bible characters and give examples from saints in church history. The definitive symbol of God is Jesus

Christ, the Word and Image of God; we have, therefore, a single, fixed symbol in Christ. In every age and every culture new symbols emerge to help us understand that one absolute unchanging symbol—Jesus Christ. For example, C. S. Lewis forged innovative symbols of Christ in his novels, such as Aslan, the Lion in the Chronicles of Narnia, or Elwin Ransom, a philologist in the Space Trilogy.

What is that to me? My mind forms the word "God" and I desire to communicate him to a friend in the Chittagong Hills. My fingers find *G-O-D* on the keyboard. Off goes a signal to etch those letters on a hard disk. I add words before and after *G–O-D*. A "send" button fires my cryptic message to a distant sorting station handling trillions of similar bytes, up to a satellite circling earth, then back down over thousands of miles to a word processor in the town of Bandarban. The *G-O-D* bytes remain lifeless alongside others on a dark disk. My friend comes in from a day helping Christian villagers cope with waters that have overflowed banks and destroyed crops. He turns on his computer. His eyes run over the cryptic message, "We heard about the heavy rains and flooding. *G-O-D* is your refuge. Can our churches help?" Those three bytes reminded him of the One who had led his people thus far. He took courage and hope. Word became symbol.

3. Helps

Aesthetics — This is a general term that refers to the visual arts. The Christian use of matter and art for theological symbolism had to overcome Hebrew abhorrence of idols and Platonic mistrust of material images. "First attempts at depicting a visual prayer were found in the early Christian catacomb paintings. In developing an aesthetic theology the delicate balance between two poles of thought had to be kept. One pole of thought said that imitation or representation leads to idolatry. The opposite view asserted that symbols are man's only access to reality and enable him to participate in it. The historic church attempted to avoid either extreme by developing an aesthetic theology.

"The church building, for example, became an image of the heavenly Jerusalem and entering the church was truly entering the City of God" (Dixon). Beauty is seen as the splendor of the divine; the icon or image does not contain the sacred but is a means for communicating with the sacred. "Beauty became the radiance of truth. This gave it moral legitimacy…number or proportion became a symbol of God…experiencing the geometric harmonies of the building was receiving or experiencing the creative act of God." Statues within the church manifested biblical drama or states of grace attained by nameless saints.

However, with the Reformation and its iconoclastic tendencies, the *logos* or manifestation of God became restricted to proposition. Art became mere illustration, "beauty became ornament...nature an object. In any creative sense, theological aesthetics died. Divorced from the image and matter, the liturgy became simple magic, or a device for the manipulation of emotion."

What is that to me? If beauty is the radiance of truth, my task is to make sure our sanctuary and the service itself befit the Creator of all beauty.

Apologetics — This is a term derived from the Greek word *apologeia* and means "the defence, by argument, of Christian belief against external criticism or against other worldviews" (Hebblethwaite). There are different avenues taken in defence of the faith. A person can "argue *philosophically* in defence of the greater reasonableness of belief in the existence of God. He may argue *religiously* in defence of the greater spiritual power of a religion of redemption. He may argue *morally* in defence of the greater moral force of incarnational belief. He may attempt to argue for the *compatibility* of Christianity with modern science, or indeed for the greater *intelligibility* of the cosmos in terms of creationist belief."

Tillich's point of departure is that Christianity answers questions arising out of the human predicament.

Barth was hostile to the use of apologetics, for he saw no common ground between Christianity and pagan beliefs. The Bible, however, presupposes man's capacity to recognize the power of the Gospel message, though pagan beliefs and attitudes cling like a veil over his heart. Christian apologists must deal with that veil. Paul's address on Mars Hill is an apologetic.

What is that to me? I openly point out weaknesses in another person's position, answer criticism of my own. A silent Christian not only lets paganism triumph, but becomes paganized himself, as were hidden Christians (*kakure Kirisutan*) in seventeenth century Japan. Buddhist icons became mingled with Christian symbolism.

Dialectics — A method of gaining knowledge of God through a process of reasoning in statements "of yes and no, of paradox, in which polar pairs are held together only in the response of God-given faith" (Richmond). Who can logically reconcile such pairs as finite and infinite, time and eternity, wrath and grace, divine sovereignty and human freedom? These pairs are brought together only in the mind of faith. God transcends "rational comprehension and, it must be stressed, dogmatic formulation."

What is that to me? Acknowledging inability to resolve apparent theological contradictions, I commit them to God. Before others I will be a dialectic, living in time and eternity, under divine sovereignty and human freedom, obeying commands but experiencing grace, working as if everything depends on me, believing everything depends on God.

Epistemology — This term refers to the theory of knowledge. It sets criteria for the limits and validity of human knowledge. Throughout the history of human thought two knowledge-strands have been emphasized: (1) the rationalist strand that stresses the power of human *reason* to grasp truth about the universe and God; (2) the empirical strand which stresses that all factual knowledge is derived from *sense data*. This second strand of thought leads to the conclusion that theology and history cannot be factual, for neither can be measured.

Immanuel Kant stressed both thinking and sensing, but added that our faculties determine ahead of time what can be known. For example, linguists stress the importance of *language* in determining our knowledge. That is, one's understanding of the universe is shaped by the language in which thinking takes place. A Spaniard and a Chinese, then, view the universe differently. From another vantage point, psychology has shown the crucial role emotions play in acquiring knowledge.

Biblical epistemology stresses the relation between faith and knowledge, love and knowledge, obedience and knowledge. It also affirms indirectly that sources of Christian knowledge are three: personal experience, revelation, and human history.

Barth stressed the unknowability of God by unaided reason: "For Barth, God creates the conditions of his own knowability by revealing himself to the faith of the believer" (Hebblethwaite). But since God's revelation is "received by human beings, expressed in human language, and tested by human reason and experience," it seems doubtful that knowledge through revelation alone, without critical thinking, is possible.

What is that to me? My knowledge of God is never complete; today I will learn more about him through scripture, prayer, the communion of saints, or new experiences. Also I have moods. As Lewis points out, "moods will change, whatever view your reason takes, I know this by experience. Now that I am a Christian I do have moods in which the whole thing looks terribly improbable . . . the first step is to recognize that your moods change. The next is to make sure that, if you have once accepted Christianity, then some part of its main doctrines shall be deliberately held before your mind for some part of every day. That is why daily prayers and religious reading and churchgoing are necessary parts of the Christian life."[3]

---

[3] Quoted by George Sayer, *Jack: C.S. Lewis and His Times* (San Francisco: Harper and Row, 1988, p.169).

History — Scripture abounds with commands to remember God's ways with his people. Israel was to establish monuments and festivals so that the new generation would learn from God's acts of deliverance, revelation, and judgment in the past. The prologue to Luke's gospel gives us four ways for understanding history. There history is seen as unique *event*, happening only once; as *research*, compiling the data; as *record*, selectively placing the events down in some sort of order; as *interpretation*, imposing some order and meaning on the chronicle of events. Because man does such organizing, he has his own bias and stands at a point of time within history; his interpretation, therefore, is always partial. In other words, the meaning of events cannot be fully understood by those within the historical process itself. Hence, the true meaning of history is fully known only by God himself.

What is that to me? I take history seriously, unlike many in the Indian religious tradition for whom history is a chain of meaningless, repetitive and fatalistically determined events out of which one should somehow extricate oneself. The law of *karma* (law of retribution) and *samsara* (cycle of reincarnation) makes history an enslaving drudgery, a burden and a prison cell. But for me, history is something to be celebrated, something to which I should contribute and make richer. I cherish history by reading and learning from it, yet temper conclusions about the grand story still unfolding.

4. Sharpeners

Philosophy asks questions about the meaning of life and attempts to clarify the human dilemma but does not give answers. It gives criteria for testing truth, such as logical consistency and adequacy to facts; it provides concepts for delineating truth, such as paradox, metaphysics, analogy, paradigm, transcendence, and immanence. Philosophy does not make truth claims; rather, it explains theology in modern idiom and sorts out truth from error by providing criteria for coherence.

Science limits itself to sense-data, searches for new facts and relations not known before, and expresses fact-relations in mathematical equations. Since science limits itself to sense-data, it can neither prove nor disprove the existence of God. Until recently, science claimed an absolutism not attained by theology or philosophy. However, science has come to realize there is a human element within knowledge; categories for classifying sense-data vary with language and culture. Hence, science has adopted a more provisional stance, one called *critical realism:* the external world is real and though our knowledge of it is partial, such knowledge is nevertheless true.

Theology takes a similar stance when talking about God. Though our knowledge of him and his revelation is partial, such knowledge is true and can lead us to salvation.

The word *science* has a variety of meanings, ranging from (1) a body of reliable knowledge divided into minor disciplines, called *sciences* that cohere into a world view, (2) a method of investigating experience through study and experiment (3) a source of power, e.g., science produces modern technology. The growth of science and technology over the last 350 years, with the consequence of science's cultural domination, has had a profound effect upon religious studies.

Most of the conflicts between religion and science are theoretical in nature — e.g., between Galileo and the church's view of the universe, creation and evolution, and more recently between intelligent design and randomness. Sometimes we Christians seize upon a pleasing scientific theory, like conflating geological periods into the "days" of creation, only to be embarrassed when the theory breaks down under further scrutiny.

Insisting on autonomy, science isolates other disciplines, including religion, into academic departments, but assumes for itself a position of dominance. Religion attempts to exempt itself from this dominance by distancing itself from the scientific method but in doing so loses relevance and slips into fantasy.

As knowledge expands, science changes, ever mindful of its limitations. For example, science cannot investigate the human mind with the same precision it does other entities. Likewise, theology acknowledges its limitations: miraculous healings are real but God uses science and circumstances to achieve them.

Science and theology need each other. Theology provides symbols and motivations for scientific investigation. For example, science has never seen "conscience," but research cannot be done without conscientious people devoted to a cause greater than themselves. Theology provides symbols for such character development but needs science to keep that training related to real life.

In many cases it is down to earth. "The Religious Experience Institute at Oxford has come to general consensus about religious experience as being grounded in external objects of encounter, not just mystical, unverifiable experiences" (Habgood). This is as we expect. The Christian church should not fear science or retreat from its institutions as American evangelicalism did in the mid-20th century.

Mark Noll explains this retreat in his book, *The Scandal of the Evangelical Mind*. He reminds us that "evangelical thought remains heavily shadowed by the fundamentalism from which it has struggled to emerge since the 1940s. The enormous weight evangelicals put on the experience of conversion, understood as a onetime, life-changing event, has drawn energies away from intellectual concerns. If one believes that the central religious drama takes place in an immediate, emotionally charged experience of God's grace, then one is not likely to devote attention to more difficult, indirect, or mundane ways in which God may be known. Nor is one likely to ponder how the converted life might be lived out in institutional settings or in the arena of politics, the arts, and the sciences.

"While admiring much of what evangelical activism has accomplished, Noll thinks the neglect of intellectual life has been disastrous. It has been a strategic mistake, because it has meant forfeiting the chance to influence the world of universities, think tanks and elite journals. These are the institutions that shape the terms of public discussion and, in turn, shape hearts and minds . . . . A determined lack of interest in studying the human and natural worlds reveals a lack of interest in God's creation—which, as Noll observes, is hardly a way of praising God. Those who think they can dispense with the study of nature and human history, believing that these realisms are not worthy of Christian interest, are ignoring the message of the incarnation and replicating ancient heresies that pitted spirit against matter and God against an evil world.[4]

What is that to me? Five nights ago, after finishing the science paragraphs above, I went to bed, only to be awakened by mild chest pains. A blood pressure

---
[4] From a review of Noll's book by David Heim, "In the Shadow of Fundamentalism," Christian Century, May 3rd 1995, p. 488 *et passim*.

check sent me to the emergency room of a large hospital nearby. After admittance to the hospital, I found myself on a table looking at green-garbed goblins in tennis shoes preparing to solve my problem. Instead of hovering over me they took their places before TV monitors and followed a thin wire probing for the injured artery. I was awake as the cardiologist guided that wire to the trouble spot, made visible by coloured dye coming from the wire. The team called out in coded terms information to help the cardiologist. It was like being in a NASA flight control room. The success of the "flight" depended upon each one's performance and they knew it.

Why would I seek for a miracle when science was performing one before my eyes. Tonight, fifty-six hours after that probe, I'm sitting back at my computer, writing this paragraph. Science and faith are the best of friends.

5. Awareness

The OT sharply distinguishes between Israel serving Jehovah and the nations serving idols. Yet, the covenant with Noah was understood as having universal dimension, and God's choosing of Israel was for a purpose—to bring God's blessings to all peoples. In the NT heathen gods are considered worthless idols, and though Gentiles have an awareness of God, salvation is only through Christ.

Yet, here again "Jesus rejected the nationalist attitudes of Pharisees, saying Gentiles would share in the kingdom and would be judged on the same basis as Jews (Braybrooke). Logos theology emphasizes that God reveals himself through Christ to everyman's conscience.

Christians regarded Islam as a Christian heresy, leading to crusades and enmity. Raymond Lull (1232-1315) was an exception. He attempted to reach "Muslims through love and a knowledge of their beliefs. Aquinas suggested reaching them through reason and natural revelation which needs to be corrected by biblical revelation." Luther edited a German translation of the Quran.

Roman Catholic missionaries who followed in the wake of European expansion in the sixteenth, seventeeth and eigthteenth centuries regarded the natives of Latin America as having minds that were a *tabula rasa*, a blank slate on which foundations of Christian truth had to be written. In Asia Francis Xavier followed this view but after encountering the Japanese, came to believe not everything in culture need be rejected. Matteo Ricci in China and Robert de Nobili in India attempted to present Christian truth in terms and concepts of Chinese and Indian cultures.

Protestant missionaries of the nineteenth century regarded other faith, religions as devil-inspired. There were exceptions, of course. Bishop Reginald

Heber appreciated aspects of Indian culture. Carey produced a Sanskrit grammar and translated the Ramayana into English. Gradually a less confrontational stance was adopted, one of appreciation and understanding. In the 20th century, study of world religions became popular, with an emphasis away from such terms as Hinduism, Buddhism, etc., which are Western terms, to the "faiths" of other people. However, right up to the present, evangelicals have insisted that "adherents of other faiths religions and worldviews . . . must let themselves be freed from their former ties and false hopes in order to be admitted by belief and baptism into the body of Christ."

Like Paul who used the word *religion* only in a negative sense, Barth took a strong anti-religious stance: "Religion as the human search for God is *unbelief*, the great concern of godless man, in contrast to *faith* which is human powerlessness before the Word that reveals the judgment and grace of God." To Barth religion is evidence of human pride and rebellion. Kraemer in his *The Christian Message in a non-Christian World* felt that people of other faith religions are "attempts by man to raise himself to the divine."

The desire to appreciate some good in other faiths, religions has led to dialogue, which stresses the "need to listen as well as to speak." The issue of salvation through Christ alone was not addressed until several missionary theologians argued that God speaks to every man in his conscience. Good Hindus may be "called" without realizing it. Karl Rahner calls them "anonymous Christians," attested by exemplary living, not cognitive awareness of Christian truth. Such eclectic theologians attempt to find truth in other religions, asserting that there are many channels of God's grace and many gospels. However, one has to decide upon a criterion of judgment in making these assertions, for such accommodating views run contrary to historic Augustinian theology and destroys motivation for Christian mission.

What is that to me? On one hand, scriptural statements say clearly there is no other gospel, no salvation apart from Christ. On the other, in human culture lies preparatory truth for the final truth revealed in Christ. Japanese people have high ethical standards and willingly participate in Christian charity. Today, Japan is a foreigners' paradise. The law of God is inscribed on Japanese hearts, and when they violate cultural norms such as honesty and filial piety, the Holy Spirit convicts, causing some to seek salvation from God. I must find them. Moreover, I need to be aware of the subtle danger of preparatory truth; some remain stuck there and in complacency fail to embrace the final truth revealed in Jesus Christ. This is true with many good religious people in India; I need compassion and sensitivity in my approach to them.

6. Approaches

Biblical Theology – This term describes "any theology which seeks to base itself largely or wholly on scripture" (Houlden). It became popular in the 1940s and 1950s in reaction to liberal theologies and "emphasized the distinctive nature of biblical concepts as opposed to their connections with the cultures surrounding Israel." Through William Albright, *et. al.,* the focus of biblical theology turned on history, stressing the fact that God acts in history and these historical acts are the medium of revelation. Cullman used the term "salvation history." Some themes developed in biblical theology were "covenant," "proclamation," and "confession."

However, even biblical theologians were selective in proving their particular theological theme—Cullman's idea of history fit more with Luke and Acts than with John. A newer approach is the attempt to understand the life of communities in which biblical narratives took place. As a subdivision of biblical theology, both New and Old Testament theologies have formed. Let's consider both:

New Testament Theology. – This theology attempts to describe the thought of the NT writers in their own terms, not 21st century ones. Such analysis makes it clear that the NT was not written to provide a comprehensive theology. The Gospels tell us a story, as does Acts. The letters are occasional, that is, prompted by local issues in the early church. Hence, the importance of a theological doctrine cannot be inferred from space given it. More space in I Corinthians is given to the subject of food offered to idols than to justification by faith. Monotheism is explicitly stated only a few times but is implicit throughout the NT.

Also the particular approach of each NT writer must be taken into consideration. Each of the Gospel writers has a slightly different theological emphasis: Matthew, for example, shows that the church is the true Israel. Paul deals with the Christian and law; the writer of Hebrews discusses the church's relation to Judaistic ritual. Yet, there seems to be a unifying core of doctrine, agreed upon by scholars of both extremes: "the NT writers' unity in multiplicity consists of their common witness to God's saving action in Jesus Christ, to his establishment of the church by the Holy Spirit, to his freeing men and women from the world for active love, and to the future consummation of that Christ-centered saving action" (Zeisler).

Is NT theology normative for the church today? Bultmann believed that it is because the Gospel calls us to authentic existence. Cullman saw in the Bible a story of the saving acts of God in history; for this reason scripture is God's timeless revelation.

What is that to me? The Bible is my basic book, the primary source for God's truth. Regularly I read, study, and meditate upon it. But I will not be bound by a fixed regimen; some days I read much, some days little. It is far better that Bible images and truth continually flow over my mind. They create a crisis of obedience; if I fail to follow biblical truth, it has no meaning for me.

Old Testament Theology—Scholarship has taken various approaches to the OT. Some scholars see it as a record of the religious experiences of sages and prophets. They, in turn, directed their message to people of their time with no thought of the future. Others place the OT on the same level as the NT by relegating OT narratives to *allegory* and by the use of *typology*. Gerhard von Rad saw in the OT a central theme of God's *covenant* with Israel which gradually broadens to include all men. Another approach is to find in the OT the "record of how God worked out the *salvation* of Israel in the concrete *events of history*, and how what he accomplished in his dealings with the men of the OT eventually found its fulfillment in Christ" (Porteus and Clements). Baumgartel finds in the OT and the NT a central theme of *promise*. God's calling of Israel is the beginning of promise fulfillment, and it is culminated in Christ who brought salvation to all mankind. And now through the Spirit, Christ indwells the believer, enabling him to reach out to mankind.

Natural Theology—If one starts with his environment, then a natural theology emerges. This theology says that knowledge of God can be acquired by man's reason without revelation. All the evidence is clear. Thus Romans 1 says awareness of God through nature renders man "without excuse." A modified view is that reason can assure us of the existence of God and other certain truths, but only divine revelation can assure us of the doctrine of the trinity, the incarnation, the atonement, etc.

Dogmatic Theology — Dogma comes from the Greek *dogma,* meaning "decree or doctrine." If one focuses on the creeds of Christendom, he will develop a dogmatic theology. In contrast to systematic theology which also embraces moral theology and apologetics, dogmatic theology focuses on core Christian doctrines — the trinity, the incarnation, redemption, sin and grace, the church, the sacraments, etc. "Dogmatic theology expresses a dialogue between the historical faith of Christians and reason. It draws on the scriptures, official church teaching, the history of theology, liturgical texts and other items which make up the lived tradition of the believing community" (O'Collins). It serves as a test or criterion for evaluating theories borrowed from allied disciplines (e.g., anthropology or psychology) which it may critically use under the control of dogmatics. Dogmatics has used reason and philosophy to "clarify, elaborate and systematize."

What is that to me? I will repeat one of the Creeds at least once a week. Under their light I will scrutinize new or speculative theologies that appear. Neither pragmatism or popularity but faithfulness to scripture and the history of orthodoxy will determine my allegiance.

Indigenous Theology — When scholars attempt to understand God and his revelation in a particular cultural context, indigenous theologies emerge. Teaching about God must be relevant to the environment in which that teaching takes place. It should answer questions raised by the life situation people find themselves in, answers rooted both in the Bible and in the situation. It is the written Word becoming flesh; as cultures change, indigenous theologies must also.

Jesus spoke Aramaic, but the NT was written in Koine Greek. This was an attempt in itself to indigenize God's revelation in NT times. Paul used words filled with unbiblical meaning (e.g., terms from Greek mystery religions like *mysterion*, *soter*, or *metamorphosis*,). In the same way the Gospel today must engage in dialogue "with such loaded words as *samsara, nirvana, dharma,* and *karma* when it expresses itself to the Hindu world" (Koyama). Extreme approaches to indigenization would attempt to use these words but give Christian meaning to them. *Dharma*, then, would not mean the Hindu law of the universe but God's principle of forgiveness through the atonement. Or, "seek ye first" could be another way of saying "give things up" which is a Buddhist ethic. Sadhu Sundar Singh said, "Hinduism has been digging channels. Christ is the water to flow through those channels."

Indigenous theology takes different forms: they can be brief commentaries on scripture or arrangements of scriptural passages that address the local situation; narratives and stories of Bible heroes can be told in modern idiom; Christian lyrics can be put to traditional harvest songs. Another form is building upon core cultural concepts, enlarging them in a Christian context, e.g., the peace child of Papua New Guinea or the Thai water-buffalo in Koyama's Water-buffalo Theology.

What is that to me? I cannot completely indigenize Christian theology or weaken Christ's uniqueness. But selective indigenization enriches Christian experience. I must make scriptural truth meaningful to my interest group or culture. For children I can develop a child theology, for athletes an athlete theology, for the handicapped a handicapped theology, for the aging a geriatric theology, in every case using appropriate idiom to focus scripture on that value system.

Moral Theology—If one begins with a study of man's sense of right and wrong, which C.S. Lewis does in *Mere Christianity*, a moral theology develops. This term is used "by Roman Catholics and Anglicans for the study of ethics and ethical questions in the light of Christian self-understanding"(Maguire). Moral theology developed from two basic premises in the NT: the proclamation that the reign of God is at hand, and that Jesus is the moral symbol of God. Moral theology is specific in the NT, as in Galatians 5:19-24, but more general in the 2nd century *Didache* (The Teaching) where the good way is contrasted with the bad. Thomas Aquinas (1224-74), considered the father of modern moral theology, believed man comes from God and through grace and moral choice returns to him. In modern times we have the rise of bioethics, addressing such issues as euthanasia, abortion, capital punishment, etc., and also social ethics dealing with structural oppression and injustice.

Process Theology — Some scholars resist the idea of basing our knowledge of God upon the past. Since he is a living God, understanding him must be a continual process. Process theology, then, is a theology which emphasizes "event, becoming, and relatedness as basic categories for its understanding rather than those of substance and being" (Pailin). The essential idea motivating proponents of this theology, held by Whitehead and Hartshorne, is that "what is real is essentially in process." God is seen as that reality "who ensures the continuation and orderliness of the process of actualization and who is the basis of the appearance of novelty through those processes." Of course, God is unchanging and absolute. Yet, as a loving God he enters into our changes to empathize with us. God suffers the pains and experiences the joys of his creation. "God is lovingly and ceaselessly active in the created order, respecting the integrity of his creatures, cherishing the values which they have produced, and motivated by the desire creatively to transform that order so it may actualize further and greater aesthetic riches."

Process theology seems to contradict bold scriptural statements such as "I, the Lord, change not." Yet, if his created beings change and he enters into their joys and pains, does he not change? This is a paradox. Perhaps it would be better to use the term *living theology*. What appears as change from man's vantage point is what happens when the God of Abraham, Isaac and Jacob walks with his people in their earthly pilgrimage. Process theology is forerunner for the "open view of God" theology advocated by some conservatives in the postmodern era.

What is that to me? As a finite being living in space and time, I understand God more clearly when he speaks in modern idiom and in the present tense. However, the One who declares himself Alpha and Omega (beginning and end) is not limited to my present, which tomorrow becomes past. God is not a being in process; he is the Being, the "I am that I am." He will always be a mystery to me, but I learn more about him in proportion to my response to what he has revealed.

7. Say that again

Anthropomorphism — The word comes from two Greek words, *anthropos* (man) and *morphos* (form or shape); hence, "form of man." Technically it is the "representation of something unlike man — the sea, an animal, a computer, or God — as possessing human characteristics" (Hebblewaite). We use anthropomorphisms rightly when we talk about God, since we are made in his image. Also the incarnation encourages us to do so, in as much as God anthropomorphizes himself in becoming man. Some anthropomorphisms, like "wisdom" and "love," seem appropriate for describing God's character. We learn these qualities from human experience, but they are derived from God who is perfect wisdom and love. Other anthropomorphisms, like "rock," "lion," "tower," "eye," seem inappropriate, yet the Bible uses them. God is not a rock or a lion or a tower. He doesn't have an eye or a hand. But his relationship with us can be best visualized in those terms.

What is that to me? Use words that keep God's transcendence and immanence clearly defined. This means avoiding colloquialisms like "the Man upstairs," "Oh, my God," or "Good God!" and instead, adopting expressions like "Father in heaven," "God of comfort," "Merciful Lord."

Apocrypha — A term meaning *of doubtful authenticity* used to denote ancient writings included in the Catholic Bible, but excluded from the Protestant one. The issue of the canon was faced by Jerome (4th century) when he translated the Scriptures into Latin. He decided to include the Jewish scriptures, called these the OT, then between the OT and the NT placed other books which he called the Apocrypha, or "not canonical." This implicitly treated them as having lesser authority. Calvin declared that apocryphal books have no authority at all. The British and Foreign Bible Society in 1827 decided not to include the Apocrypha in their Bibles and this greatly affected their lack of use by Protestants.

What is that to me? If I refer to any apocryphal book, as did Amy Carmichael on occasion, I will remind listeners it is not part of the original canon.

Canon — A term which came from an Egyptian word meaning a "reed used for measuring." It means in today's parlance, "rule" or "standard." Not until Athanasius used it in the 3rd century was the word used regarding an authoritative list of sacred writings connected with the "new dispensation in Christ . . . it was only gradually and in a piece-meal fashion that the canon of NT scripture grew up" (Hanson).

Catechism — The process of making divine revelation known to seekers in a way that nourishes faith is called *catechesis*, from which we get the word *catechism*, a manual for oral instruction. Paul hints that such a manual existed in the 1st century when he used the Greek term *tupon didache* (pattern of teaching) in Rom. 6:17. "The object of catechesis is . . . to lead people to communion with Christ, to build up the community of believers, and to strengthen the missionary activity of the church . . . the context of the catechesis was the liturgy, its method was preaching, its content was both doctrinal, based on the creed, and moral—the twofold law of love and the commandments" (Konstant). "There are four sources of catechesis: scripture, doctrine, liturgy and experience. Liturgy is the way the believing community expresses its faith in worship. Experience has to do with the context within which faith takes root . . . the opportunity for continuing catechesis throughout life should be available to all Christians." That is, there should be forms for instructing children, adolescents, the elderly, etc. "All members of the church take part in the work of catechesis according to their particular gifts and responsibilities."

Gospel—A word derived from the Greek word *euangellion* that means "good news." It is a general term that speaks of the benefits proclaimed in Christ. In Mark, the gospel ushers in the reign of God in human hearts and abrogates the reign of sin. For those who receive the gospel, it demands renunciation of sin, endurance under trial, and honouring Christ in one's vocation. In Acts, the gospel is the missionary proclamation "of the kingdom of God and of Jesus as Christ and Lord" (Grayson). In Romans it declares

Jesus Christ as God's Son and our Lord by his resurrection. It also discloses God's righteousness to those who believe.

Hermeneutics — A term derived from the Greek word *hermeneuien*, meaning "to interpret." That word originally came from the name "Hermes, a messenger of the gods who makes intelligible to human beings what otherwise cannot be grasped" (Mudge). It is translated "means" in Hebrews 7.2, "explained" in Luke 24:27. Paul is called Hermes in Acts 14.12. Hermeneutics embraces both exegesis, the determination of the original meaning of a text, and "exposition, the elucidation of its sense for modern readers." Hence, hermeneutics is a broad term used for explaining the meaning of a scriptural passage within a particular cultural context.

Kerygma — A Greek word meaning either "what is proclaimed" or "the act of proclaiming." In theology it has two meanings: (1) the "single original core of the Christian gospel within the varied NT writings" (Evans). This has usually meant the Pauline preaching of the Cross and Resurrection, but also includes the pattern of preaching in Acts 2-13: (2) "the announcement of salvation in and through particular events (not processes or ideas) interpreted as decisive acts of God."

Tillich contrasts *kerygmatic* theology, i.e., theology that gives the core message of the Bible, with answering theology, i.e., theology that answers questions people have when they relate the eternal word to the historical moment. But even *kerygmatic* theology used conceptual tools of the time, words such as *sophia, logos, plerurna, mysterion.* The continuous task of theology is to work out a synthesis of the original core message with its relevance in the modern cultural context.

What is that to me? I must present the gospel in a way my hearers understand: use intelligible idiom, imageries and concepts, without obscuring the original gospel message. Good knowledge of scripture and familiarity with contemporary idiom are a must. Newspapers, journals, novels should have a significant place in my daily reading.

Parable — A term from the Greek word *parabole*, meaning "a placing beside or a comparison . . . at its simplest the parable is a metaphor or simile drawn from nature or common life, arresting the hearer by its vividness or strangeness and leaving the mind in sufficient doubt about its precise application to tease it into active thought . . . in the NT a parable was not an interpretation of scripture but a tale drawn from images and similes of ordinary life. It invites the hearer to discern a secret inner meaning which has some analogy with the story as told but stands on a quite other level than its obvious surface meaning" (McFague).

Parable and allegory have one thing in common: they both indicate that biblical texts may have double meanings: "the surface expressions are a coded representation of a hidden and more spiritual meaning . . . parables, like fables, allegories and myths, are stories with hidden meanings, but they have the following characteristics: *mundanity, extravagance,* and *indirection.* As *mundane,* the parables imply that the rule of God applies to secular, ordinary and in many instances, relational life, both personal and public. As *extravagant,* the parables imply that the ways of the conventional world are not the ways of God . . . there is tension between the logic of merit and the logic of grace. As *indirect,* the parables imply that their significance must be grasped in a shock of recognition as listeners apply the stories to themselves. They tease the imagination into participatory thinking. Jesus was "the parable of God who upset the conventions of the world and sided with the oppressed, the outcast, the sinner."

The interactive partners of parable signify two ways of being in the world — the way of the conventional and the way of the kingdom. "The action in a parable is indicative of the *kerygmatic* quality of parables, for they are the paradigms of persons encountering the kingdom, not abstractly, but concretely and existentially."

Typology and Allegory — Typology is a comparison of historical events or persons along a scale of time, such as Adam and Christ or the Exodus and the Cross. Allegory, on the other hand, is not historical; it makes a biblical text into an indicator of eternal truths. Typology is Jewish; allegory is Greek.

The basis for both typology and allegory is found within the Bible itself. John the Baptist comes as the new Elijah; Jesus, the new Moses. Early Christian expositors began to find in the NT fulfillment of OT prophecies. Others took this double-meaning concept further by stressing timeless principles behind historical ritual, such as baptism replacing circumcision: "allegorization was a process of universalization: it stripped away, for example, the elements in Sarah's position (cf. I Pet. 3) and extracted an element which was morally lasting" (Barr). In other words, Sarah was to be an example to Christian women. Names of places in the OT also took on an allegorical significance within Christian literature, e.g., Jerusalem as the "vision of peace."

Typology and allegory, then, underscore the fact that religious practices gradually change into new forms for expressing timeless truth (such as drama instead of preaching), but scripture itself is tied to the historical milieu in which it was written. Early Christian expositors like Origen (cir. 200 A.D.) attempted to expound the entire OT allegorically. The Reformers, however, rejected allegory. Modern expositors do not use the term allegory but actually look at scripture in two senses: the linguistic/literary sense and the religious/theological sense.

What is that to me? I appreciate the role of parables, typologies and allegories in effective communication. But I take care. If I allegorize the parable of the Good Samaritan into rescuing the parish from financial malfeasance, it will resonate with the vestry but not with the core message. Modern allegory must be based upon sound exegesis.

THE FATHER

8. The Almighty

Springtime comes early in the southern reaches of the Yangtze. Beginning in February huge cloud-columns pick up speed, then race overhead, their silent rush punctuated by thunderclaps and lightning. Overcast weather returns for a spell until suddenly a washed-out sky unveils distant blue ranges. Yesterday's leaden cover bursts in frenzied movement today--towering cloud masses on the march, announcing the advent of spring or summer.

On this unforgettable day, as late afternoon showers poured down, out from boiling black clouds shot hundreds of lightning bolts through the sky, great white shafts that bridged heaven and earth. Before Peng a rainbow rose from the Yuanshui River, then arched out to the Wukong Range. Like black peonies, numberless small clouds wafted along, variegated in colour from white to grey to black. Out of every flower core emerged filaments, bundles of light, each a different shade. Peng stood on the brow of the hill, lost in admiration at the brilliant sky dappled by three-dimensional peony-like clouds. Words could not portray that flamboyant scene, those dancing black clouds pierced by shafts of light. The riot of colour racing by epitomized life's evanescence. Yes, thought Peng, as the Chinese proverb has it, "No matter how fierce the fire blazes in the field, its smoke vanishes like a puff in the sky. Yet, the beauty of the moment emblazoned on our memory triumphs over the ephemeral" (*Return to Chaos*).

For people without the Bible, like the above Chinese prisoner, from time immemorial such displays of nature transport them from the mundane to the sublime, but rarely to belief in a Divine Creator. That truth has been suppressed by idolatry. However, once faith takes a person to the Creator, everything falls into place: morality, responsible behaviour, natural law, ecology, stewardship, etc.

Thus, it is no accident most theologies describe God first in terms of his essential nature — who he is, then describe him in terms of his acts — what he does. For example, the Apostles' Creed, begins with the words, *I believe in one God, the Father, the Almighty* (his nature), *maker of heaven and earth* (his acts). Erickson develops the doctrine of God under similar categories: the Greatness of God (his person) and the Goodness of God (his acts in the world.) The *Thirty-nine Articles of the Church of England* define God as follows: "There is but one living and true God, everlasting, without body, parts or passion; of infinite power, wisdom and goodness; the maker and preserver of all things both visible and invisible"

(Robinson and Shaw). Biblical faith in God asserts his uniqueness, meaning that "God alone is the ultimate authority in human life and the ultimate refuge amid all the perils of historical existence." Since God is the ground and source of life, claims of all other gods are false.

In the fourth century, Augustine borrowed from Plotinus in asserting that God is the source of all being and knowledge, the One from whom all things derive their essence and existence. But Augustine cautioned that "the human mind is so darkened by sin that human beings could not of themselves ascend to the Truth. Accordingly, he consistently taught that we can learn only by grace and must believe in order that we understand." Leaders of the Reformation differed in their overall perception of God. For Luther, God is our heavenly Father; for Calvin, our sovereign Creator.

In the modern era, Tillich suggested three ways for interpreting the word *God*. The first usage is one that separates God as a being, the highest being, from all other beings, alongside and above which he exists. He created the world and stands above it as moral administrator. This is a primitive view and the one most generally held. Its weakness is that it makes the infinity of God merely an extension of finite categories. Children perceive God as being like a loving grandfather, Santa Claus, a wise professor, or even superman.

The second usage is one that identifies God with the universe, with its essence and special latent powers, e.g., the Great Force. This is naturalism which destroys the transcendence of God by confusing him with the created world. It neglects the attribute of holiness in God, for holiness puts God at a distance from his creation.

The third view takes the word *God* as a symbolic representation of the Creator-Lord of the universe. He is the ground of all being, yet transcends everything. It follows, then, that whatever we know about a finite thing, like the sea or mountains, or art, we can know about God, for he is the ground of beauty, laws, etc. Nevertheless, whatever we know about a thing cannot be fully applied to God because he is transcendent. This third view has much to commend it.

What is that to me? Modern day Hinduism is a vast, far-reaching tent under which broad, even contradictory, religious traditions co-exist. Those traditions are distinguished by names, such as Jainism and Brahmanism, or by a distinguishing philosophy, such as monism, dualism, polytheism, pantheism, animism or even atheism. Each religion has an ultimate reality to which a name is given. What unites all these religions is this: in most cases they adopt the word *God* for translating their ultimate reality into English. Thus when I use the word *God* in a Christian context, I must be clear about its meaning. I do this by explaining biblical passages that describe God's person and work, then by living out Godlike qualities—holy, loving, just, compassionate, forgiving.

9. Looking

Since we have never seen God, and our finite minds cannot fathom his infinity, how do we find him? Theologians take two approaches:

Look within yourself—Schleiermacher, the father of modern theology, began with man's *feeling of absolute dependence.* Once a person acknowledges his dependency and frailty before a vast universe, he is not far from theistic belief. Immanuel Kant also looked within man, but seized upon a different facet. He believed human understanding was limited to sense experience. This makes it impossible for man by rational proofs to come to a knowledge of God. Instead, Kant postulated a moral order in the universe and a *moral imperative* over man. Knowledge of God, then, begins with a sense of "I ought." In other words, ethics is the point of departure for knowing God. True virtue, Kant taught, must act whatever the consequences. When those consequences lead to a persecution of the good, the final answer to such a situation must be found in God himself, who ordains the complete good.

Tillich began with man's experience of God, an experience determined by culture. This may seem vague, but once a Westerner immerses himself in Eastern culture, he becomes empathetic with the difficulties Asians have in understanding the God of the Bible. In the Far East a consistent humanism, as expressed in Confucianism and Shintoism, makes it difficult for Chinese and Japanese to grasp the concept of a transcendental God active in creation and history.

Look outside yourself — Augustus Strong believed knowledge of God begins with an assumption that he exists. Once we make that assumption, everything else falls into place; the world makes sense. Aquinas felt that all of creation affirms God's existence; we learn about him by observing his creation. Karl Barth began with special revelation; unless God reveals himself to man, man remains in ignorance. God reveals himself through his acts and his names.

The different Hebrew names for God tell us much about him. He is *El*, the strong and mighty one. Throughout the OT, *El* is used in the "intensive plural" (*Elohim*) to signify God's fullness and power. He is *Elyon*, the high and exalted one. As *Adonai*, he is the Ruler and Lord to whom everything is subject. He is *El shaddai*, the all-sufficient One who distributes bountifully to his creation. He is *Yahweh*, the eternally self-consistent One who enters into covenants with his people and does not change. He is *Sabboath*, the glorious One.

In summary, both the OT and NT tell us that God is *spirit*: invisible and without parts. He is a person, capable of having a relation with human beings. He is living, the self-existing one. He is infinite, not limited by space or time. In relation to man, God is holy, righteous, just, faithful, loving, and gracious.

10. Proofs

Throughout church history four "proofs" for the existence of God have emerged:

The Cosmological Argument of Thomas Aquinas moves from the dependent character of the world, to God as the non-contingent source. If we suppose an endless number of cars on a train track we finally discover the engine. Every effect has a cause. Modern theologians have taken exception to the Thomist view of First Cause, pointing out that creation is dynamic and God is continuously involved in his world.

The Teleological Argument moves from the orderly and designed character of the world to a divine designer. "The physical universe is not a chaos of random events but a system functioning in accordance with universal regularities or 'laws'" (Hick). When we find a watch, we presuppose a watchmaker; when we observe the human eye or the ozone layer of the universe which filters out harmful rays, we assume there is a Creator. This reasoning was not questioned until David Hume, the 18th-century English mathematician, raised objections to the teleological argument. He postulated that random particles over an infinite length of time will fall into an order that will account for the universe as we know it. Darwin's theory of natural selection seemed to support this claim. Though Darwin himself was a believer, his followers took the theory of natural selection to its unintended conclusion. Their modern counterparts would say, for example, that God did not put enough ozone above the earth to protect man; rather, only those creatures who could survive with that much ozone to protect them from the sun's rays did. In modern times the teleological argument has come back into vogue through an emphasis on intelligent design. In its defense, creationist scholars stress the high improbability that random atoms could form together molecules necessary for life. Such order-through-randomness would require much more time than the present calculated age of the earth.

The Moral Argument says that "The universe has produced ethical animals. Must there then not be a transcendent moral source or ground of our moral nature? . . . . The existence of God is a necessary presupposition of the absolute claim upon us which moral obligations have. When I ought to do something, this 'ought' is unconditional." Against this theory, sociologists hold that moral laws were developed by human societies as a necessary condition for harmonious social interaction. Those laws were then internalized as conscience. Such a position, however, does not take into consideration Emile Durkheim's view that moral laws precede, not follow, the development of society.

The Ontological Argument— The word *ontological* comes from the Greek word *ontos*, meaning "existence." This argument was formulated by Anselm (1033-1109), who held that God is "that which no greater or more perfect can be conceived." The fact that we can imagine a Perfect Being means he exists. Against this reasoning some have said that just because a person imagines an idyllic island in the sea doesn't mean it exists. Tillich's reasoning seems more germane: people who argue against the existence of God because of war, sickness, famine, etc., evidence an internal, absolute standard by which they judge all religious claims. That is, they are presuming a more perfect Absolute exists. From whence did this Absolute come?

The above four arguments are not compelling to the modern mind. Furthermore, they are weakened by the notion of existence itself. "Existence" is a term used in distinction to non-existence. A tree exists in the sense that at one time it did not. When we say God exists, we say this in contrast to non-existence. But God does not exist; he is the ground of all existence. "We can never guarantee God's existence by defining Him as existing; in the words of W. H. Auden, 'All proofs or disproofs that we tender of His existence are returned unopened to the sender.'"

11. Denial

What is Atheism? — A belief that there is no God. There are many forms this belief takes. Some deny the existence of God on *linguistic* grounds. A. J. Ayer expresses it: "Since it is impossible to define God in intelligible terms, then one is allowing that it is impossible for a sentence to be both significant and to be about God" (Sutherland). Some point out the lack of compelling *evidence*. All the good in the world is out-weighed by the evil: "The evidence of our flawed world and the random play of forces in our universe suggest that there is no benevolent purposive creator at work." Such a flawed world causes some like the character Ivan in Dostoyevsky's *The Brothers Karamazov* to say, "If the price of eternal harmony is the suffering of children, then too high a price is asked for harmony." Some 19th-century thinkers denied God on *psychological* grounds: Feuerback said, "the personality of God is nothing else than the projected personality of man." Marx felt that "man makes religion to suit his own goals." Freud asserted that "belief in God is a projection of wishes." Some modern theologians like Tillich are critical of *anthropomorphic* tendencies within classical Christianity: "It is as atheistic to affirm the existence of God, as it is to deny it." His point was that use of the term "existence" denies God's transcendence and makes him merely higher than the rest of creation. Lastly, many people subconsciously adopt an atheism of *indifference,* evidenced by their lifestyles and concerns. "Alasdair MacIntyre: 'The creed of the English is that there is no God and that it is wise to pray to him from time to time.'"

What is Polytheism? — A belief in many gods. Virtually all religions except Christianity, Judaism and Islam are polytheistic. However, philosophy tends to support monotheism, for the notion of "God as a self-subsisting being or pure act cannot admit of multiplicity"(Shorter). The idea of equilibrium among gods is an absurdity, and venerating one god while worshipping others means the others cannot be God. There is little evidence of development from polytheism to monotheism; cultural artifacts demonstrate the reverse: proliferation of functional deities from original monotheism. Because man desires a unifying core of reality, among major religions of the world it is difficult to identify a philosophical concept of polytheism. The real in Hinduism is the *non-duality* of Brahman; in Buddhism it is *sunyata* or "emptiness;" in Chinese philosophy it is the *li*, organizing principle of the universe. In conclusion, the history of human thought demonstrates that polytheism does not satisfy man's quest for transcendence. He begins to seek a unifying core in transpersonal concepts, returning to original monotheistic belief: from the One to the many, then back to the One.

12. Creation and Providence

Creation — This doctrine asserts "that every existing thing depends upon God for its existence" (Habgood). Creation, a corollary of belief in God's sovereignty, rejects the theory of randomness. John Blanchard, for example, in his book, *Does God believe in atheists?* notes that Roger Penrose, who developed *black hole* theories, "estimates as one in one-hundred billion to the 123rd power the odds of a Big Bang producing by accident an orderly universe as opposed to chaos." Blanchard quotes useful analogies about the likelihood of the universe allowing for the existence of life, such as hitting a target an inch wide on the other side of the universe. Of course, even if the universe by chance came out right for human purposes, we would need a livable home in space. Earth's size, distance from the sun, and rotational speed had to be just right. We need the air above not only for breathing but to protect us from cosmic rays and meteorites. We need light (but not too much ultraviolet), and so on. What about the origin of life? A chance of one out of 1,000,000,000,000,000 is considered a virtual impossibility, but when DNA co-discoverer Francis Crick calculated the possibility of a simple protein sequence of 200 amino-acids (much simpler than a DNA molecule) originating spontaneously, his figure was 10 with 260 zeroes after it."[1]

In a world where much is mysterious, painful and threatening, the doctrine of creation must be accepted by faith. Such faith is vindicated at the cross where God accomplished his purpose in the face of evil and death. "Creation stands secure because God's faithfulness has been demonstrated at the Cross."

What is Cosmology? — This term means literally, "reason about the world," and is used to sum up one's view about the nature of the universe. Gnostic cosmology viewed the world as evil. Some Greek philosophers believed the "real" to be unchanging, while others believed reality was always changing. Buddhist thinkers took the latter view. Ancient Chinese thinkers saw a universal order behind the visible; it was man's task to move harmoniously with

---

[1] Marvin Olasky, *World Magazine,* April 14, 2001, p. 50.

that cosmic order. In contrast to the above cosmologies, "Christian cosmology holds that the world is a product of divine activity . . . that God acts on the world to create it and redeem it" (Alderlink). Two facts flow from this hypothesis: (1) the world cannot be divine; nothing in it is a proper object of worship; (2) the world is subject to God, and therefore "rational, orderly and patterned." Theology lives with the paradox that the world is moving according to God's pattern, yet man is responsible for acts within it.

What is that to me? Since the world is created by God, I will be actively involved with it. Withdrawal has no place in a Christian cosmology. True spirituality does not deny the world or escape from it. For me Mother Teresa is a shining example of a 'secular spirituality.' As a faithful steward I protect the environment, I uphold the family, I support the government.

What is Providence? — "By providence we mean the continuing action of God by which he preserves in existence the creation which he has brought into being, and guides it to his intended purpose."[2] It refers to God's *foreknowledge* and *governance* over creation. Believing in God's providence enables us to face the future confidently, knowing that things are not happening by mere chance. We

---
[2] Erickson, *Christian Theology*, I, p.387.

can face danger, knowing that he is aware and involved.

Theologians have distinguished God's *general* providence, sustaining his creation, from his *special* providence, intervening in nature and history for special purposes. God's general providence includes not only preservation but also government, moving events toward an end.

Why pray? If God is guiding events in the world, why, then, should the Christian pray? God not only wills the end but also the means which include our prayers. We participate with him in his providence by prayer and action.

Prayer to God was spontaneous from Israel's earliest history. "The Psalms exemplify direct approach to God, the pouring out of concerns for the harvest, safety, deliverance, forgiveness, and the giving of thanks. Jesus added an intimate dimension to prayer by using the word, *Abba* (Father). Christian prayer is to be done in the name or Spirit of Jesus, who makes intercession for the believer. Such prayer is also corporate, even when we pray alone, for it is the church praying through us; my concerns are the concerns of my brother and vice-versus" (Richardson).

This rules out all selfish requests and every attempt to manipulate God. "The essence of prayer is not asking but offering, not self-seeking but self-dedication: not my will but thine be done." In contrast to the Jewish cultic of his day, Jesus stressed that prayer to the Father should be private, conversational, brief, frequent and intense.[3]

Evangelicals are uncomfortable with scripted prayer in worship, but historically the church has adopted Psalms and NT passages for corporate prayer. Paul, in his great exultation in Philippians 2, was probably quoting a 1st century hymn. Far better that public prayer be written out ahead of time, easy to follow, than be extemporaneous and rambling.

What is that to me? At communion, why should I improvise when Thomas Cranmer's prayer has stood the test of time: "All glory be to thee, Almighty God, our heavenly Father, for that thou, of thy tender mercy, didst give thine only Son Jesus Christ to suffer death upon the cross for our redemption; who made there, by his one oblation of himself once offered, a full, perfect and sufficient sacrifice, oblation and satisfaction, for the sins of the whole world ... we, thy humble servants, do celebrate and make here before thy divine majesty, with these thy holy gifts, which we now offer unto thee, the memorial thy Son hath commanded us to make; having in remembrance his blessed passion and

---

[3] See F.D. Bruner's *The Christbook, Matthew 1-12*, Wm B. Eerdmans, 2004, pp.281-291.

precious death, his mighty resurrection and glorious ascension; rendering unto thee most hearty thanks for the innumerable benefits procured unto us by the same" (*Book of Common Prayer*).

Does God interfere with his own laws in answering our prayers? To answer this, we must rid ourselves of popular misconceptions about God such as "the man upstairs." He answers our prayers, but often not in ways we choose. Jesus could not work miracles in some towns because of people's unbelief. "There is much to be learned from the so-called unanswered prayers of Jesus (Mark *14.35ff*)."

What are Miracles? Theology has supplied various answers: (1) miracles are seen as manifestations of unknown natural laws. This view strips miracles of their divine quality; (2) miracles are seen as breaking natural law (such as the axe head floating or Jesus walking on water) for the twin purposes of meeting human need and giving credibility to prophetic utterances; (3) God brings into play another law which supersedes an existing one to accomplish his own purpose. An example would be God's overcoming death with life in the resurrection.

What is that to me? Providence is sufficient; I need not seek miraculous intervention, for he daily intervenes through family, friends, events and medical technology. But let God be God. He intervenes through miracles at his good pleasure.

Often in India miracles occur in areas where faith is strong and medical technology weak. I personally know people from tribal areas who have come to personal faith in Jesus Christ through his miraculous deeds on their behalf or their communities. I neither demand miracles from God nor question his direct intervention when they occur.

13. Grace

What is Grace? An English translation of the Greek word *charis* which, depending on context, has three distinct meanings in the NT: *graciousness, special empowerment,* and *undeserved favour.* This last meaning harks back to the Hebrew *chesed* of the OT which signified not only God's redemptive love towards undeserving sinful men but his sustained determination to maintain that relationship to them. In Greek culture *charis* did not have this *undeserved favour* meaning. Trench says: "There has often been occasion to observe the manner in which Greek words taken up into Christian use are glorified and transformed, seeming to have awaited for this adoption of them, to come to their full rights, and to reveal all the depth and the riches of meaning which they contained, or might be made to contain."[4]

---
[4] This quote and others on *grace* are from my *Biblical Encounter with Japanese Culture*, Christian Literature Crusade, Tokyo, 1967, pp.86-87.

Charis, he says, originally signified that property in something which excites joy in hearers or viewers of it. Later in Greek usage, it denoted the gracious aspect of beauty—"the gracious or beautiful thing, act, thought, speech, or person it might be, itself—the grace embodying and uttering itself." Then it signified "a favour freely done, without claim or expectation of return." This aspect of the word is taken up by the NT and used to denote the freeness of the gift and the unworthiness of the recipient. *Eleos* (mercy) had to do with misery, pitying the miserable; *charis,* with forgiving. "We may say that the *charis* of God, his free grace and gift, displayed in the forgiveness of sins, is extended to men as they are guilty; his *eleos* as they are miserable."

With this dominant meaning *grace* pervades the NT. The same grace manifest in God's dealings with his covenant people is now manifest in Jesus Christ. His character, life and work can all be summed up as an appearance (*parousia*) of grace. Furthermore, the resurrected and exalted Christ is considered a repository of grace for those united to him by faith. Thus Paul employs the term "grace which is in Christ Jesus." Arndt's definition succinctly expresses this concept of NT grace: "The context will show whether the emphasis is upon the *possession of divine grace* as a source of blessings for the believer, or upon a *store of grace* that is dispensed, or a *state of grace* (standing in God's favour), that is brought about, or a *deed of grace* wrought by God in Christ, or a *work of grace* that grows from more to more." Those who tap this reservoir of grace not only remain in a state of forgiveness for daily sins, but this grace actively produces in them the stamina, powers and capability for active mission. Hence peculiar gifts of preaching, teaching, leadership are called *charisma* – grace gifts. From start to finish, the NT economy is one of grace.

Faith, repentance, sanctification and service – these visible responses to divine acts of grace on our behalf are not traced to some spark which kindles attitudes and actions befitting God's condescending acts; rather the responses themselves are traced to a secret inner working of God, vouchsafed in grace.

What is that to me? How thankful I am that grace (*krupa* in Sanskrit) is a fundamental property of the Triune God, flowing to me when I fail, and pervading every work he blesses. If I were to subscribe to the doctrine of *Karma* (the law of retribution) then I can neither fault others when I am victim, nor thank anyone when I am victor, for I am the fated captain of my soul, maker of my destiny. Merit or lack thereof determines my estate in life.

Contrariwise, as a Christian, gratitude is my response to God's grace; and that gratitude is demonstrated when I am gracious to others when they fail.

THE SON

14. Incarnation

"I'm delighted to meet you," began Suzuki, bowing with hands on a low table in the *tatami* room. "Shin told me about you. Your time in Manchuria. Battles you fought in China, Indonesia, and Okinawa."

"Oh, that. It's all behind me now. Have some tea and *osembei*," offered Yuki. "Shin asked me to meet you. I'm a Buddhist but don't go to the temple. Nor to the shrine. I've never been to church. Shin wants me to break out of my isolation, make new friends. I'm not motivated. Perhaps it was the war…"

"If I went through what you did, I'd feel the same," consoled Suzuki, trying to a get a purchase on the problem.

"Kazuko and I are surprised," continued Yuki. Shin has changed since he got faith. But I'm too old. How can faith change the past? I find no meaning in what I went through. That's why I avoid people and mistrust government. I'm content with my job and family."

At that moment Kazuko opened the sliding paper doors, and from a kneeling position placed bowls in front of each one. Suzuki looked down at the steaming rice topped with cooked egg, onion and chicken. Taking chopsticks in hand, he began again.

"Nakajima san, you grew up on a farm. You sowed rice and reaped harvests. Rice grains produce more rice by falling into the soil, allowing their hulls to disintegrate, to die. It's a life principle. Jesus used the grain metaphor to prepare his followers for an apparently devastating defeat, his death on a cross. He told them that through his sacrificial death God's glory would be revealed."

"Glory?"

"Yes, the word means brilliance, majesty, power. God would somehow bring light out of darkness. Er,...triumph out of defeat, strength out of weakness. Jesus knew this and lived with the sign of the cross over his heart."

"Which means?" asked Yuki.

"He never lost sight of the life principle—his death would bring life to the world. And in accepting the humiliation of the cross he experienced the presence of God, his glory."

"He had a choice, I didn't," protested Yuki.

"You do. I do. When life disappoints us, we can withdraw, nursing our wounds. Or by faith turn defeat into victory and allow new life to spring forth, a life that is outgoing, caring, vulnerable" (*Return to Chaos*).

A seed falls into the soil, the shell crumbles, green sprouts appear, yellow grain ripens. In Part III, we watch the same drama from Incarnation to Resurrection. The great Kernel disintegrates on earth and appears again in another form — the Church.

What is the Incarnation? It is a word derived from the Latin *incarnatus* made up of two roots — *in* and *carno*, or "in flesh." Theologians use the word to describe the act by which God who is Spirit took upon himself flesh and blood in order to fully identify with the human race. "The readiness of God to subject himself to the conditions of mortal life, to take suffering and evil upon himself to the point of the cross makes belief in him much easier than any other argument ... over against law, religion or ritual, the Incarnation has become the permanent channel of man's relationship to God. Moreover, God's own self-involvement in the world of human suffering and sin becomes the pattern and the inspiration for Christian ethical commitment, at every level of individual, social and political involvement" (Hebblethwaite).

What is that to me? In the Indian context we see some similarities but more dissimilarities between *Incarnation* and the Hindu doctrine of *Avatara* (descent or appearance). Incarnation is God's intervening in human history once-for-all in an act of human redemption. In contrast, avatar appearances are temporary, a fairy-like phantasmagoria, happening in a variety of forms, some human, some animal, for the purpose of protecting the righteous by destroying the wicked. Therefore, though I may use the word *avatara* to indigenize incarnation, I must stress the uniqueness of the Christ-event.

What is Arianism? — A belief held by Arius, a 4th-century Alexandrian priest, that Christ, as the created Son, is subordinate to the Father. The key phrase, "There was when he (the Son) was not," summarizes Arius' desire to maintain a strict monotheism. Jesus then becomes a secondary being. Arianism was denounced as heresy at the councils of Nicea (325) and Constantinople (381).

What is the Imitation of Christ? — The person of Christ in the NT is the keystone of Christian ethics. In using the title Son of Man, Jesus saw himself as a model for Israel. He completely walked in the way of the Lord, always doing those things that pleased the Father. Paul exhorts his followers to imitate him inasmuch as he imitates Christ. This has to do with self-abnegation, obedience, and love. He then spoke of the work of the Spirit in our hearts to bring about this imitation. During the Middle Ages there were attempts to reproduce the acts of Jesus in the life of the Christian, following the stations of the Lord's life in the liturgy of the Mass. Luther at first followed ideals of Bernard of Clairvaux, but later reacted against such attempts. He saw in them a doctrine of works. Eventually, Luther abandoned the word *imitate* and used instead *conform*.

What is that to me? Imitating Jesus Christ and being conformed into his likeness challenges me to the core of my being: can I, as an imitator of Christ, invite others to imitate me just as Apostle Paul did? This is the real test of my spirituality. Models of Pandita Ramabai of Mukti Mission, Mother Teresa of Kolkata, Mrs. Gladys Stains of Baripada, Orissa and many others challenge me: "Oh, Lord, help me. This is my prayer."

15. The Cross

What is the Theology of the Cross? This is a Pauline doctrine derived from the phrase, "the word of the Cross." The formulation of this theology can be traced to Luther who contrasted it with the Catholic theology of glory in his *Heidelberg Disputation* (1518). The theology of the Cross says that "God is known in the Cross of Christ and experienced through suffering" (Moltmann). God reveals himself not fully in creation or human works but indirectly and in a hidden way. In contrast, God is known explicitly, says this theology, "through suffering and Cross . . . the Cross is the criterion of all things . . . the Cross signifies not just Jesus' death, but the whole of his life which stands under the sign of humiliation." This concept is traced back to the OT where God reveals himself indirectly through the Suffering Servant. God's mercy is for the oppressed, the hungry, the prisoners. Anglican theology has renewed this emphasis on the Cross with its teaching that God suffers and endures pain with his creation. The heart of the triune God is involved in the Cross and in the Eucharist. Theologians from all traditions — Protestant, Catholic, and Eastern Orthodox — are saying the same thing. At this point there is unanimity: Jesus' divinity is seen in his humiliation. "The Son offers himself and endures dying in being abandoned by God on the Cross; the Father leaves the Son, offering him up and suffers the death of the Son in the pain of love." The theology of the Cross completely reverses worldly criteria for success: power, wealth, fame. Instead, it becomes the "sharpest attack on all political idols: *the crucified God* calls, as the God of the poor, the oppressed and the humiliated, for a demythologizing of all earthly authorities, and frees men and women to follow Christ in faith, love and hope."

What is that to me? The Cross of Jesus Christ amazes me; in powerlessness I find strength; in ignominy, glory; in suffering, joy. Power is self-denial, glory is vulnerability, greatness is servanthood, joy is sacrifice. Alexander the Great, Caesar, Napoleon, Adolf Hitler, Joseph Stalin, Pol Pott, Idi Amin, and other 'strong men' of world history continue to attract many, but the charm of Jesus Christ, Mother Teresa, Father Damien, and Gladys Stains is not to be seen in them. Whenever words like *success, achievement, acclaim* enter my mind, the Cross deletes them.

What is Redemption? It is the English translation of the Greek word, *apolutrosis,* meaning "buying back." In the original social context it implied that an individual or society has been brought under some kind of bondage. " A person may become a slave of another, or a nation may be under the subjugation of a foreign power, or a person may be under some demonic possession. In Israel's case the people found themselves under bondage to Egypt and could not redeem themselves. Hence, they were continually reminded that it was Jehovah who had redeemed them. The same was true of deliverance from Babylon. Yahweh was their Redeemer" (Dillistone). Slave markets and exchange of goods for persons was common in the first century. NT writers seized upon the "redemption" simile to express what Christ had done for mankind. We are left in no doubt that the great deliverance has been achieved; that it was a costly process involving the precious blood of Christ; that its benefits (freedom from bondage to sin, the law, and demonic powers) can be appropriated by faith; and what now is enjoyed in part by the redeemed will receive its fulfillment in the age to come."

When the metaphor is pressed into literal details, e.g., to whom was the ransom paid, etc. difficulties arise. "The central theme represented by such words as redemption, deliverance, liberation, is that of divine compassion leading to active succor on behalf of those oppressed and unable to help themselves . . . by identifying himself with humans in their temptations, trials, hopelessness, suffering and death he paid an immeasurably costly price and brought into being a new humanity, bearing his own image and committed to following his example."

What is the Atonement? It is an English word which originally meant *the condition of being at-one*, used to express harmony or reconciliation after two parties had been estranged from one another. Soon a secondary meaning emerged: *atonement* denoted the means, such as an act or a payment, through which harmony was restored. It occurs in Romans *5:11* as translation of the Greek *katallage* which literally means "downing the otherness." In other NT passages this Greek word is translated "reconciliation" (II Cor. 5:18).

How did Reformers like Luther and Calvin use the word? "Luther made the leap of faith to believe that Christ had touched bottom on his behalf — the sense of the uttermost reaction of divine righteousness to human sinfulness — and in so doing had brought about 'at-one-ment' between man and God such as no agencies, human or divine, could destroy." Calvin, imbibed with theories of Roman law, stressed Christ's work — both his life and his death — as substitutionary for the sinner, securing atonement between sinful man and a holy God.

16. Resurrection

What is the Resurrection? The act of rising from the dead. It is the English translation of the Greek word *anastasis*, which literally means "to stand again." The Gospels do not describe the resurrection. Rather, they emphasize its outcome: the empty tomb. Jesus' resurrection is a central theme in the NT, for it overcame all obstacles to our being what God intended the divine creation to be. It became God's basis for man's purpose in life, possession of the Spirit, full life, ethics. The historic church believes in the resurrection because Jesus did. He spoke about it and with parables taught that human behaviour in this life determines the nature of life in the next. Secondly, resurrection is rooted in the very nature of God. "Would it be divine love to create us with immense spiritual potentialities that cannot be fulfilled?" (Hick)

Caroline Bynum traces the development of belief in bodily-resurrection in her book *The Resurrection of the Body in Western Christianity, A.D.200-1336*, Columbia Univ. Press, 1995. "She focuses on the period from 200 to 1336, the year Pope Benedict the XII declared that souls experience the beatific vision, with the resurrection yet to come. Preachers and theologians pride themselves on avoiding body-soul dualism, but pious talk at funerals is usually of the departed person surviving as a vague, benign spirit or as a thought in the memories of others. The early church did not follow gnostic tendencies of the period, that is, they did not accept dualism or hate the body. Similarly, despite its suspicion of flesh and lust, Western Christianity did not discount the body. Indeed, person was not person without the body. Over against the modern preoccupation with the body as the locus of sexuality, for most of Western history the body was understood primarily as the locus of biological process."[1]

That being the case, what sort of change takes place between the earthly and resurrected body? In what way were the two the same? The church's concern was to assure the identity of the resurrected and earthly body. "Resurrection victory over death had to be a triumph over putrefaction, the scattering of the martyred body. During the second millennium

---

[1] Kyle Pasewark, reviewer, *The Christian Century*, 1995, p. 404, *et passim*.

the fundamental significance of the body remains constant. Resurrection is never reduced to a question of the soul. Even accepting the beatific vision concept, the soul doesn't lose the particularity it had when associated with the body. That is, the soul becomes almost body-like. However, Paul stressed change, the transformation of a living, changing organism. By the twelfth century, Western thought reached its materialistic and literalistic apogee. Pauline language about what was sown in corruption being raised incorruptible is generally understood to mean that the material bits of this body are replaced and rendered incorruptible in the resurrected body. Eucharistic theology provides part of the support for this position as early as the late second century and continues to do so through the twelfth century. Eucharistic eating reverses the usual process of nutrition. Normally, digestion transforms consumed food into the property of the consumer; in contrast, the body of Christ begins to change its consumer into Christ's being. That is, the dominant mode of thought has been in terms of material continuity and reassembly. Augustine believed that although matter need not serve the same function or be placed identically in the resurrected body, the matter itself is nonetheless identical."[2]

---

[2] Kyle Pasewark, *Christian Century,* 1995. p. 404.

In NT times among members of the Qumran sect and the Pharisees, resurrection referred to the final action of God whereby he would resolve the contradictions of human life, discriminate between good and evil, and permanently establish a righteous elect. That Jesus was raised means that God has already begun that process. Yet, since the end has not come, the resurrection of Jesus "gives rise to new things in the present, having the quality of resurrection: a universal mission (the Gospels, Acts, Paul's epistles); a relationship with God available to all by faith; a community of the elect entered by baptism; this baptism is a present union with Christ's death to sin and anticipates a future union with his risen life; a possession of the Spirit which is an earnest of final glory; a life which has passed through judgment and is eternal in quality" (Evans).

What is that to me? Death is not the end; there is resurrection, judgment, and everlasting life. Therefore, my life on earth is not to be spent in eating, drinking and making merry, but in living for him and others. In the face of death I take courage in Jesus' words, "I will raise him up at the last day."

17. Christology

What is Christology? It is an inquiry into the significance of Jesus for Christian faith. Such faith is not about Jesus but faith in Jesus. Belief in God is directed towards the man Jesus. "The man is not the same as God: he speaks of his Father in heaven. He is not good, but only his Father is perfectly good. He is and remains a man, and still participates in the life, thought and action of his Father. He is at the same time the glory of God and the glory of man" (Newlands).

    The task of Christology is to express the full "divinity of God in the man Jesus, showing how he is both truly God and truly man ...to avoid the confusion that would make Jesus neither fully divine nor really human." Throughout church history Christology has oscillated between divine and human poles: the Docetists (a 2nd-century heretical sect) saw Jesus' existence as appearance *(dokein* means "to seem.") At the other pole, the logos Christology of Justin Martyr stressed that Jesus was "the eternal and universal Logos of God from which all order and rationality were derived." Arianism held that Jesus was the incarnate Logos. As such, the "Logos suffered in Jesus, while God remained unchanged. Arius' theology was indeed a theology of the incarnation, but the incarnation of the Logos rather than of the Creator in the created order." Nicaea made it clear, however, that Jesus was equal with God, of one substance with the Father. Finally, the debate was settled at the Chalcedon Council *(451 a.d.)* which said, "We confess one and the same our

Lord Jesus Christ, the same perfect in Godhead, the same perfect in manhood, truly God and truly man, the same of a rational soul and body, acknowledged in two natures, without confusion, without change, without division."

In the twentieth century, Chardin developed his cosmic Christ concept. The Catholic theologian Balthasar in his *A Theological Aesthetics* expanded this concept by showing "how the form of the incarnate Christ, the pattern of his life and death and return, can be seen as the norm of beauty and thus the hidden goal of desire in a vast range of religious and cultural phenomena, pre-Christian and post-Christian: all human art is drawn magnetically to that point where the finite world in all its helpless tragedy is transparent to the beauty and glory of God. These pairs-intelligibility and beauty, understanding and love – unite in the vision of the central revealed image of Jesus. Christo-centrism, then, is the logical outworking in history and art of Paul's declaration, 'For me to live is Christ.'"

MAN

18. Christian Anthropology

Chinese defenders evidently got wind of a Japanese relief column headed for Kairikyo. When the new moon silhouetted Yuki's unit against an abandoned farmhouse, snipers opened fire. Yuki leaped into an open ditch, but Tanaka kept moving against another fusillade that swept across the field. Yuki saw several men fall. Through the dust and confusion a searchlight probed for moving forms. When the blinding light passed Yuki, he knew his moment had come. Over the ditch he leaped and raced for the fallen men. *Tanaka! Not you!* He bent close to check Tanaka's vital signs. *Ah, still breathing!* Next he cut away the reddened area of the shirt. *In the shoulder! Above his heart!* Yuki then tore off cotton swaths to staunch the bleeding. *Here comes the searchlight!* He held Tanaka tightly and feigned death.

When the searchlight moved on, Yuki threw down his pack and positioned himself under Tanaka's limp body. With one stupendous effort he stumbled forward, Tanaka piggyback, pack in hand, and made for the ditch. Within minutes relief units caught up with them. Yuki pressed two men into getting Tanaka back to the first aid tent at Shinsochin. As medics examined Tanaka, Yuki collapsed on a cot nearby. *Why so exhausted? Hello! What's this? On my arm? Blood oozing from hair follicles?* He grabbed a small mirror from his pack and looked again, rolling up pant legs. *Not only from arms but legs.* He opened his mouth and stared. *Sure enough, gums are red and sore. That's it! Scurvy!*

Auxiliary units around Kairikyo were checked by the dogged defenders and could advance no further toward Nanking. As medic-in-charge Yuki was ordered to accompany the severely wounded, including Tanaka, back to Shanghai and home to Japan. In Osaka a medical checkup determined that because of scurvy Yuki should be de-activated. It appeared that his war days were over. The growing appetite of the military meant he could serve his country just as well farming. Yuki went on inactive reserve status, returned to Nagano and began assisting his father in rice cultivation.

Later Yuki learned about General Matsui Iwane and his troops as they advanced toward Nanking in December of 1937. General Tang's soldiers scattered before them in a pell-mell rout that swelled to maniacal panic as the fighting neared the gates of Nanking. A report of what ensued — the Rape of Nanking — came from Japan's Foreign Minister Hirota Koki after his inspection trip in January 1938: "The Japanese army behaved in a fashion reminiscent of Attila and his Huns." Was this an example of military discipline sliding into stupefying depravity? Or did the whole setting unbridle the demons in men's souls? Or was it an eruption of a culture permeated with martial competitions, samurai ethics and the code of Bushido? Yuki knew something had gone tragically wrong (*Return to Chaos*).

In this section we penetrate the soil into which the divine Kernel fell. The depths of depravity to which man has fallen, as shown in the vignette above, demonstrate the need for divine intervention.

Anthropology comes from two Greek words, *anthropos* (man) and *logos* (reason), and means "study of man." Christian anthropology, if indeed there is one, though borrowing from empirical science, gives anthropology depth of meaning. It says man is *created*, the object of God's purposeful love. Its *body theology* upholds the "permanent integrity of the human body as given in creation, affirmed in the incarnation of Jesus Christ, nourished in the sacraments of the Christian churches, and to be glorified in the resurrection of the body" (Nelson). It articulates "personal and social attitudes toward the body, moral decisions regarding one's own body, and concerns for physical conditions in which people live and work."

Man is *culture-creating* in history, performing acts that coincide with God's creative and redemptive purposes. Furthermore, man is *social* and *political,* not merely individualistic; church life is his model. Body theology affirms man's *human sexuality* and with it *erotic love. Social equality* is anchored in God's acceptance of all persons without discrimination. *Linked to nature,* man is responsible for its protection and ecology. Yet, he stands above nature as a *religious being* with awareness of the holy. Man is a *moral being,* yet *"unfulfilled,* frail and to be completed by resurrection life. He is *fallen,* leading to disorders in the self and society but *recoverable* through the perfect man, Christ" (Dyson).

What is Culture? There are many definitions of culture, one of which is "the sum of all that has spontaneously arisen for the advancement of material life and as an expression of spiritual and moral life—all social intercourse, technologies, arts, literature and sciences" (Burkhardt) or "the artificial, secondary environment which man superimposes on the natural environment. It comprises language, habits, ideas, beliefs, customs, social organization, inherited artifacts, technical processes and values" (Malinowski).[1] In summary, culture is "a corporate undertaking in which people succeed in establishing a distinctive style of living based on common values" (Jenkins).

---

[1] A quote from *Area of Light,* ISPCK, New Delhi, 1998, pp.17-18.

God imposed order upon creation through Adam, who, as its steward was offered "an apparent freedom to manage his own life without reference to God"(Jenkins). The result is that man is cast out of the garden. Work became "not the enjoyment and celebration of God's gifts but a painful struggle for survival." Throughout Israel's history she "becomes vulnerable to cultural complacency which besets all settled societies, forever turning faith into culture-religion. The essence of Israel's original faith "lay in her dependence on her Lord and her continual openness to fresh disclosures of his will from the one who is only really known in the commitment of venture into the unknown. Once that openness was lost, Israel had no barrier against cultural assimilation to the nations around her and no distinctive purpose, no power of self-criticism."

In contrast, the true people of faith in the OT sought "for a city with durable foundations, which they never identified with the earthly Jerusalem." The lessons about culture are clear: we must always love our Lord more than the cultural gifts given to us. Jesus grew up within Jewish culture, yet rejected the cultural forms by which Israel expressed herself. In fact, these cultural forms became barriers against entering God's kingdom. Paul also rejected these cultural forms. For him, "the possession of the gifts of the Spirit means a rejection of the old patterns and a new outburst of cultural creativity."

In his classic work, *Christ and Culture*, Richard Niebuhr critiques the historic church in its stance before secular culture, such as *antithesis* (Judaistic); *assimilation* (Roman Empire); *synthesis* (Medieval Catholic); or *transformer* (Reformed). The latter view was held by Augustine, Calvin and Maurice. This view says that the church must always remain in tension with both its own Christian culture and secular culture, challenging them, changing them to conform to the will of God as revealed to those involved in ventures of faith. This will of God is always in harmony with the cross and resurrection of Christ and truths emanating from them. Diagrammed, the stances would look like this:

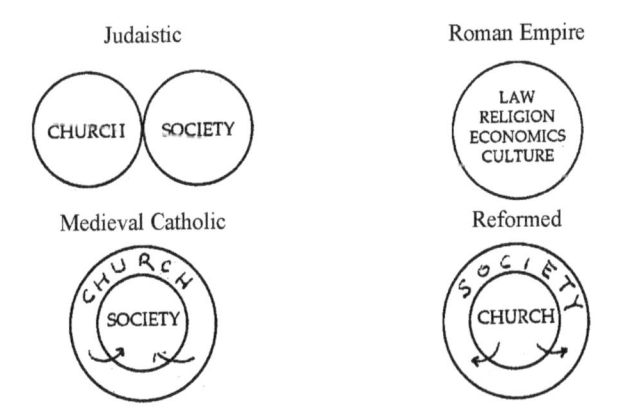

Judaistic

CHURCH SOCIETY

Roman Empire

LAW
RELIGION
ECONOMICS
CULTURE

Medieval Catholic

CHURCH
SOCIETY

Reformed

SOCIETY
CHURCH

The Judaistic or people-of-God concept was espoused by Tolstoy in 19th century Czarist Russia. He refused to have anything to do with state institutions. The civil religion view of the Roman Empire surfaced in Protestant liberalism with its view that the spirit of

Christ permeates all humanitarian institutions. Church activity is merely one of many that God uses for the good of mankind. The Catholic synthesis approach enabled its missionaries to "baptize" non-Christian practices and build upon them.

The Reformers took a different stance. From the different metaphors used by Jesus to describe the Christian's relation to the world (e.g., salt, light, investor, builder, etc.), from the teaching of Paul, from the many accounts of the early church's stance before civil authorities, Calvin, *et. al.* concluded that the church, as a subculture within the larger social sphere had a mandate to transform secular institutions by her message and life.

According to the Reformers' model, the church will grow in secular society if her members excel in all four kinds of human action — economic, cultural, social, and political. By doing this the church will provide a model for secular society and equip her members with ability to upgrade life in the community. The church has never been a gated-community; her members have continued in the secular world as artisans, workers, professionals, to meet their economic needs. Neither has the church maintained a law-enforcement system to sustain its norms. But she has been a sub-culture with her own systems of beliefs, values and expressive symbols. As the individual Christian is shaped by these cultural components, as he internalizes the church's system of beliefs and values, he becomes a change-agent in society, a transformer of culture."[2]

We understand the tension between Christian and secular cultures by borrowing three terms from Tillich: *autonomy, heteronomy, and theonomy*. These terms differentiate ethical forces or cultural imperatives under which man finds himself. *Autonomy* or law-of-the-self is an inner drive for meaning; it causes man, as bearer of universal reason, to create culture. Children do not wiggle toes in the sand; they make sand castles (*autonomy*).

Once man creates culture, he wants to absolutize it, but in so doing, meets resistance. I like my castle better than sister's. She prefers her own. *Heteronomy* or other- law is at work. When sister reacts and topples my vaunted sand castle, daddy intervenes; the three of us create a grander castle. *Theonomy* or divine-law is at work. Social science calls these three interacting forces *thesis, antithesis,* and *synthesis* but does not identify the source of these inner drives: God himself. As he protects us from sickness by the immune system, he protects us from social chaos by *theonomy*.

At the national level, *autonomy* can go tragically wrong and create a vacuum readily filled by *heteronomy*, such as authoritarianism filling the

---

[2] *Ibid,* p. 12-14.

vacuum-like nihilism of post World War I Russia with bolshevism and Germany's Weimar Republic with nationalism. Then, *theonomy* comes into play, driving man beyond these "isms" to the source of beauty, truth and justice—God himself—through people like Dietrich Bonhoeffer, Alexander Soltzhenitsyn and Vaclav Havel in Eastern Europe.

Contemporary examples of *theonomy* at work abound: in China, Maoist state socialism, after the abuses of the Cultural Revolution, was diverted toward state monitored capitalism by Deng Xiaping and his followers; in India, Nehru/Gandhi's state-monitored capitalism was given air to breathe by BJP's laissez-faire policies. In America, socialism vis-a-vis capitalism gives way to compassionate conservatism.

There will always be tension between new cultural symbols (*autonomy*) and old (*heteronomy*), but when the best of both is preserved *theonomy* is at work, melding them together into something that liberates man. In a new burst of freedom, emerging autonomy creates stresses in the economy and the environment, thereby calling forth a new heteronomy: civil unrest.

What is that to me? I will not suppress an inner drive for meaning, or be discouraged when resisted, but watch theonomy at work, creating what I could never do alone.

19. Postmodernism

In the twenty-first century the church comes face to face with an unseen, un-coded, leaderless heteronomy called *postmodernism*. To understand postmodernism we go back to the Enlightenment (1650-1800) which threw off clerical domination in every sphere of human endeavour and "stood for autonomy, nature, harmony, and progress. Though the Enlightenment may have been anticlerical and opposed to organized religion, it nevertheless exuded the confidence that God's in his heaven; all's right with the world."[3] In place of tradition and religious authority, human reason became enthroned as arbiter of truth. It was the Enlightenment that ushered in the *modern* era (1800 to mid-20th century) during which Darwinism and higher criticism called into question core doctrines of Creation and Incarnation. However, the modern era, gliding along on the twin rails of moral imperative and scientific inquiry, turned in a new direction. We are now in the *postmodern* era.

Predictably, postmodernism challenges Creation and Incarnation. Not directly, but through its assumptions. "The genesis of the word *postmodern* can be fixed with some accuracy — probably in the 1930s in Europe. In contrast to the

---

[3] Roderick Leupp, quoted in *Area of Power*, ISPCK, New Delhi, 2002, pp. 2-3.

Enlightenment and Modernism, post-modernism is nihilistic and atheistic. It denies the possibility of universal moral precepts, rules, and principles; instead it stresses a multiplicity of perspectives. It is pessimistic in its hopes, is holistic in spite of being radically relative and pluralistic, stresses the local and communitarian, and doubts that there are any over-arching or unifying myths or narratives. Popular culture films and music are often postmodern."

Postmodernism is not a movement but rather a pervasive spirit of our age. It permeates Western thought as Brahmanism does Eastern. *Brahman* is the impersonal mind of the universe, the great *It*, the all-embracing Neuter of the universe to which no adjectives can be affixed, for that would limit Brahman. From *It* derive no absolute values, history has no meaning, and the goal of man is emancipation from nature and human bondage. The term *Brahmanism* covers popular and philosophical Hinduism. The latter took the form of *Vedanta Monism*, a philosophy that blurs distinctions, reconciles contradictions and absorbs man into *Brahman*. Postmodernism is the Western form of *Vedanta Monism*, a defining vagueness, a studied imprecision that characterizes those who left or forgot their Christian heritage.

What is that to me? Be less vague, more precise. Never say "Yes" when you mean "No." Affirm the good. Admit the bad.

20. Evil

Out of sight behind the smokestack Matt unrolled several blankets on the wooden deck, stretched out a lanky frame, and lay wide awake, allowing his thoughts to fold back upon themselves. Towards dusk, haze in the air cast the ship in lurid yellow light; the drowsy murmur of faint voices brought needed sleep. Before midnight, Matt was awakened by steps on the deck. He looked into the darkness and saw a pinprick of light increasing as footsteps grew louder. It was Smitty. "Move aside! The stench below is too much." Matt obliged, then couldn't get back to sleep.

"Smitty!"

"What? I'm trying to sleep."

"Does evil exist?"

"Why do you ask that?" replied Smitty, poking his head outside the blanket.

"I can't believe it," continued Matt. "One assassin's bullet sends nations clawing at each other, pulls me away from Ohio and lands us on this wretched deck. Ferdinand's assassination, Kaiser's broken treaties were not the cause. Something more sinister is behind all this."

"Evil has no existence of its own," Smitty offered, "just like cold and darkness. Look!"

Into the dark Smitty pointed his flashlight at the smokestack. Grey metal appeared. "See?"

"What's that got to do with evil?" queried Matt, sitting upright.

"As darkness is the absence of light, and cold the absence of heat, so evil is the absence of good. When men turn from good, evil happens" *(Return to Chaos)*.

This is a theological conundrum. If God watches over his creation, how do we account for the presence of evil? For those who have no faith, evil is no problem; it is the way things are. David Hume, the 18th-century mathematician, struggled with the problem of evil. He asked, "If God is willing to prevent evil but not able, then he is impotent. Is he able but not willing? Then he is malevolent. If he is both able and willing, whence then is evil?" (Richardson). There are four approaches to the problem:

Evil as non-being—This is Smitty's approach above. Some philosophers deny the existence of evil by considering it *non-being*. Thomas Aquinas borrowed this idea from Plato. God is the source of all perfection; descending from him in a chain we fall into imperfection and finally non-existence. "Evil is nothing in itself; it represents only an absence of good. There is, therefore, in fact no problem of evil at all" (Richardson). Another form of this idea is Hegel's view that evil is an *illusion*. It is the backdrop for good, like the way dark colours of a painting set off light ones. Without the black we couldn't see the light. This view gives little comfort to a bereaved parent.

Dualistic view of evil — At the other end of the scale, some thinkers not only affirm the presence of evil but make it a force equal to the good. This is the *dualistic* view of Zoroastrianism which sees the world as a scene of struggle between light and darkness, good and evil. However, there cannot be two ultimate principles of reality. C. S. Lewis expresses it: "The two powers, the good and evil, do not explain each other. Neither can claim to be the ultimate. More ultimate than either of them is the inexplicable fact of their being there together . . . each of them is in a condition, finds himself willy-nilly in a situation; and either that situation itself, or some unknown force which produced that situation is the real ultimate. You cannot think of good and evil locked in combat without smuggling in the idea of a common space in which they can be together. Furthermore, the difficulty with dualism is that it gives evil a positive, substantive, self-consistent nature like that of good. What makes good better or more preferred than evil? Good becomes a mere matter of taste . . . a sound theory of value demands something different. It demands that good should be original and evil a mere perversion; that good should be the tree and evil the ivy . . . that good should be able to exist on its own while evil requires the good on which it is parasitic in order to continue its parasitic existence."[4]

Despotic view of evil — A few theologians approach the problem of evil from God's side. They emphasize God's omnipotence. What God wills is right because he wills it. This *despotic* view of hyper-Calvinism was renewed by Barth who refused to discuss the problem of evil. "If God is God, how can we dispute his wisdom in making things the way they are?" (Richardson) There is no problem of evil: what is, is right and good because God wills it. This view loses sight of the compassionate fatherhood of God, grieved when his children do evil, pleased when they do good. Also, "the idea that a thing is right because God wills it rather than it is willed by God because it is right will appear offensive to the moral sense of Christians."

Moral theory of evil — In contrast to the view that God's power is limited, or that it is absolute and constitutes right and wrong by decree, is the view that "God's power is limited by his own character of righteousness, truth and love." This *moral theory* says that God is limited by his essential being. He cannot will that two and two equals five; neither by the nature of goodness can he "create beings who are

---

[4] C.S. Lewis, *God in the Dock,* Grand Rapids: Wm. B. Eerdmans, 1970, p. 22.

instantly free and good... goodness, to be good, must be freely chosen; value must be freely loved in order to be attained. God in creating mankind desired to bring into existence beings who can freely choose the true, the beautiful and the good, and above all who could freely return the love which he had lavished upon them. The creation of a world in which this end was possible involved three things which constitute the problem of evil: pain, suffering, and moral evil." We know the biological utility of pain; without it we would destroy ourselves. Suffering, when bravely borne, is character-forming. The world is a school of manhood and womanhood. What we construe as evil may be part of God's plan for conforming us to the image of his Son. Concerning moral evil, we see ourselves in a predicament created when we rebelled against God. It leads to war, crime, terrorism and senseless violence. We know that we ourselves are "the problem of evil and also that through the unmerited grace of God the problem has been solved ... the ultimate solution of the problem of evil must lie in the fact that the God who created the world is also the God who has redeemed it; the Creator is himself in Christ the bearer of all creation's sin and suffering as he is the bringer of the redemption that shall be." The moral theory of evil seems to square with scripture and is what most Christians intuitively believe.

21. Pilgrimage I

Postmodernism creates a purposeless and meaningless social malaise wherein man finds himself *alienated*, a term used by Christian anthropology to express *estrangement*, a brokenness between God and man, and between man and man. The way out of it is a process, a pilgrimage that begins with warnings of:

Stage 1 — Conscience, English translation of the Greek *suneidesis,* meaning *moral consciousness.* "Conscience serves as a guide or monitor of life, enabling the individual to evaluate and choose potential courses of action and thought in the light of his or her values and commitments. For Christians, the conscience is not the sole guide to moral life; rather, informed by scripture, nurtured by grace, inspired by the Holy Spirit, and enacted in love for others, the conscience serves as a flexible yet fallible evaluator of one's own actions in light of one's understanding of God's will" (Rambo).

Stage 2 — Calling, that internal voice or external circumstance God uses to bring us out of estrangement into a relationship with himself and others. God called Moses, Samuel, the prophets and the people through them. In the NT it is an invitation to enter the kingdom, participate in the blessings of salvation, enjoy the peace of Christ, and live in freedom. Simultaneously, one may be called to a specific task. God's call "is to be received and obeyed in faith, and those called out of darkness into light are to evidence their calling in a manner of life"(Davies).

Stage 3 — Conversion, a biblical term that sums up proper response to God's calling. When I obey God's call to himself, I am *converted.* The word *converted* is a translation of two Greek words — *epistrein* or *metanoia. Epistrein* is an action word, meaning "to turn, to turn again, or to return." *Metanoia* is an attitude word, meaning "change one's mind" or "repent." Both words connote "the alteration that is made in people's lives when they turn from idols to the living God" (Rambo). Conversion has a wide range of meaning in contemporary times: transition from one religion to another, e.g., from Hinduism to Christianity; transition from one denomination to another; transition from secularism to a religious group; an intensification, i.e., "the deepening of feeling experienced by individuals who change from nominal or apathetic members of a religious group to ones whose religion is a central part of life."

Stage 4 — Faith, English translation of the Greek *pistis,* a term used in Greek society to convey faithfulness to one's word. In the religious sense, *pistis* expressed reliance upon divine oracles. This paved the way for its adaptation in the OT and NT. In Judaism, the word meant loyalty and obedience and was tinged with a sense of merit; the faithful are those who have fulfilled all the commandments and as such come into a special bargaining position with God. However, the NT "baptized" the Greek word *pistis* with its own meaning: in general it meant "turning towards the God disclosed by preaching."[5] It has the following range of meaning: put faith in the words of God; obedience to revelation received; trust in a person, or his help; loyalty; hope in something that is not quickly discernible or predictable.

Though the word embraces these aspects, it had the technical meaning of *faith in the message about Christ* — the missionary message which declared what God had done in Christ. This faith or faith's object is summed up in the Rom. 10:9 formula, recognizing Jesus as Lord and accepting the miracle of the resurrection. Stating the resurrection as part of the credal statement of faith was not to the end of eliciting mental assent, but because it is the fact upon which Jesus became Lord. That brief formula expresses the whole gamut of the work, death, resurrection, and lordship of Christ, making all the object of NT faith.

Thus accepting the NT *kerugma* was accepting the central figure of history whose person and work establishes Jesus as Lord. It involves a personal

---

[5] Rudolph Bultmann, "Faith," in *Key Bible Words* (New York: Harper and Row, 1960, III, p. 62).

relationship with this Lord, just as *amen* in the OT embraced a personal relationship with Jehovah. NT faith is linked with terms such as repentance, forgiveness of sins, obedience. Hence, "in every case, *pistis* is seen to be the act in virtue of which man separates himself from the world and turns around completely towards God in response to God's eschatalogical deed in Christ" (Bultmann). And this faith is not static, ending once admission to the Christian community has been achieved. Faith is active. Believers are the believing ones, "constantly relating themselves to God's act of salvation." Thus some may be weak, others strong in faith, according to personal growth. Faith is worked out in each life.

Though faith is the dynamism for Christian living, by no means can it be subsumed as a work of man. Works do not lead to salvation; to the contrary they lead to pride and status establishing. It is a continual proclivity in man to rest in some personal accomplishment, even his strong faith. But Pauline faith is a rejection of anything but childlike trust in the finished work of Christ. It is an expectant faith, not in the gnostic sense of escape from life but living in continual submission to the saving acts of God in Christ. John stresses faith, not as a renunciation of this world, but as a "shattering of the world's criteria and appraisals. John employs the preposition *in* more than *unto*, for he emphasizes this personal intimate aspect of faith: to believe in Christ is to come to him, to love him."

For Luther the work of Christ is giving us the gift of saving faith, which is not belief about Christ, but confidence in God through Christ. Surrendering to Christ begets faith in God. Such confidence in God comes not through a piece of information provided by authoritative scripture, but rather through the recognition of God's fatherly face. Calvin was more to the point when he used the metaphor *spectacles*. He believed the Bible functions as a lens that focuses a picture: in it the true image of God is presented, and through it God can be recognized everywhere else. This presupposes that a confused vision of God is already in the human heart.

"The great picture of the crucifixion is a supreme example. It has every appearance of a tragedy or a failure. So why then have Christians always found in the story such a powerful source of faith? It speaks of the price of redemption but also becomes a powerful statement of meaning and purpose that incorporates tragedy. The words, *Father forgive them,* is already a victory before resurrection. In short, the crucifixion narrative awakens faith because it has become a story about faith. Calvin asserted that it was Jesus' cry of faith in which he beheld the presence of God. Faith, then, is seeing God in the midst of agonies of human existence.

"Jesus evidently did give saving faith to his first disciples. Their picture of him as the Christ has continued for two millennia in the hearts of believers.

What is crucial for the picture of Christ, if it is to qualify as a historical symbol, is not that it corresponds to the life once lived by a particular individual but that it exists, embodied in the corporate life of the Christian community, as the sacramental Word by which the community is continually recreated. This is what makes it possible for faith to happen, to occur as an event of the present."

Stage 5--Justification, a term used in the NT to describe the status of those whose sins have been forgiven. It is translated from the Greek word *dikaiosune,* and "refers not to moral quality but to standing in the eyes of the judge or court. To be justified is to have the verdict of just or righteous passed upon one. That no one is justified by his own works is expressed by the formula, justification is by grace, through the redemption that is in Christ Jesus and that the righteousness of faith is the righteousness of God" (Gerrish).

Augustine saw justification as an infusion of grace that makes us righteous by pouring into our hearts love for God. "In consequence of the infusion of charity, the Christian is enabled to perform meritorious acts; he makes progress in righteousness, and what is still lacking, God forgives." Aquinas saw that justification was the effect of grace transmitted in the sacraments. Luther thought of Christian righteousness as consisting in two things: "both a healing or making righteous and a forgiving or counting righteous." It is this justification which properly establishes the basis for human works in God's economy—not a striving after salvation but the fruit of a new relationship with God.

22. Pilgrimage II

Stage 6—Adoption, the English translation of the Greek *uiothesia,* used in Roman society to connote legal acceptance of both minors and adults into another family. Those adopted received full rights of inheritance. The five NT occurrences of the word speak of a new relationship we have with God through Christ. The emphasis, however, is not on legal aspects of adoption but more on the personal. "The believer, freed from sin and fear by Christ, is no longer a slave but, by adoption, a child of God, who cries, *Abba, father*" (Davies). Through adoption we become joint-heirs with Christ. Adoption in this life, however, is not complete; it will only be completed when our bodies are fully set free from sin and death.

Stage 7—Perseverance. The Greek word is *upomone,* translated into English as "endurance," "patience," or "perseverance." It "denotes the gift of persistence in faith and the preservation of believers to the very end of temptation and persecution" (Moltmann). The doctrine of perseverance is derived chiefly from Romans 8:31-39 and directs "the believer to God's reliable faithfulness and does not leave his future open to uncertainty: God remains faithful to his election, his covenant, and his creation." Augustine in his controversy with Pelagius (4th century theologian who believed man could achieve salvation by his own power) insisted that even faith was a gift of God, stemming from God's election. The believer will continue to the end because God is faithful to his choice in election.

By the medieval period this doctrine seemed to restrict human responsibility and morality; hence some Catholic theologians asserted it was possible to forfeit the state of grace. Luther took a mid-position, believing it was possible to lose faith, since moral sins could drive out the Holy Spirit. Most reformers, however, held fast to Augustine's view, since their emphasis was upon justification through grace alone.

In summary, the perseverance doctrine has been upheld, "not as an expression of irresponsible self-assurance" but one of Christian hope. We are to understand Christian faith not as a habitual state (as in the Middle Ages) nor a decision (as in modern times), but essentially as faithfulness to God on the basis of his own faithfulness" (Moltmann).

Stage 8 – Character. In both the OT and NT, love or *agape* is central. It is the primary requirement and guide for conduct and character in Christian ethics. "Love, with the associated themes of loving-kindness and grace, mercy and forgiveness and above all fidelity, forms a constituent and constant feature of Yahweh's covenant commitment to Israel. God's love of humankind transcends all boundaries. It requires and empowers a human response to God and the neighbour" (McDonagh). This divine love was enacted in history by Jesus. Jesus' love is to be our standard for loving our neighbour. Through concern and sensitivity, love gives the other person freedom to realize his potential, "to overcome obstacles and be healed of injuries. The letting-be of the human other, loving him into his own potential and for his own sake, is the human reflection of the divine activity of creation – letting-be. When we love God for his own sake, it is letting God be God. The other side of divine love is not-letting-be. The Lord disciplines those he loves."

Once we enter the kingdom, we need training in righteousness. Such training may seem the opposite of love. Careful balance of *letting-be* and *not-letting-be* within a circle of family and friends can only be maintained by the Holy Spirit.

It is debated among theologians "whether *agape* (love) can be expressed in specific rules of action or can only be determined in the situation (the so-called 'situation ethics' debate)" (Childress). What limits *agape* are situations in which there aren't sufficient resources to meet everyone's need. Who receives our love and who doesn't? Or, when the use of force against one's neighbour is required to protect another neighbour? Must love be held in tension by justice? Or should love transform justice into mercy? Considering its positive effects in character development, is justice a form of love?

Stage 9 — Witness. When saving faith is understood as a gift, Christian witnessing becomes as natural as breathing. We *become* what we claim to be — Christians. God uses our character to engender faith in the faithless. The word *witness* is a translation of the Greek *marturos*, from which we get the word, *martyr*. Early Christians did not witness *to* others but witnessed *before* them.

The word *decision* in the Christian West sums up the moment of coming to faith. Dutifully, I brought that concept to post-war Japan. In my faltering Japanese I would ask mystified tent-meeting attendees to make a *decision* (*kesshin*, "make up one's mind"). How gratifying to see so many hands raised! How chagrined later to learn they were just polite, showing appreciation. Commitment to a person they had never met or understood was furthest from their minds. Behind the scenes, however, the real work of evangelism was going on. An 18-year old Christian girl, working in our home, methodically brought seekers to her room where they learned to pray and sing hymns. Over time, one after another bought Bibles, began attending worship and fellowshipping with Christians. Before we knew it, faith came.

Though living in the same geographical swath we call *Asia*, Indian people have a religiosity not found in China or Japan. They respect all religions and will give any a hearing. The Indian government greeted the 2nd millennium with postage stamps commemorating Christ's birth: one, an Indian artist's portrait of Jesus; another, scriptural words, *love one another*. In 1993, a stamp appeared commemorating the arrival of Baptist missionary William Carey two hundred years before. It showed the great Bible translator sitting at his desk, pen in hand. Mother Teresa received the 4th national funeral ever. Army trucks lumbered through Calcutta streets garlanded with huge crosses of yellow flowers. Martyred Australian missionary Graham Stains was raised to national prominence when his wife, on hearing the news, cried out, "I forgive them."

Should not this orientation to the supernatural be called *amorphous faith*, faith without structure or content? Into this milieu honest, caring Christians come. Their presence is *the* witness. Through the dust and din of Indian life — work stoppages, bus strikes, power outages, water shortages, scores of educated unemployed replying to one job advertisement after another, today's stress about tomorrow's rice —

genuine seekers walk with Christian friends and see faint outlines of Christ on the Indian road. They pick up their pace. They run. Faith comes. They offer for baptism.

Stage 10 — Salvation. The Greek word is *soteria* which means "wholeness" or "salvation." In the gospels salvation is in the present, synonymous with entering the kingdom; healings that took place were signs of salvation. This present-tense usage demonstrates that biblical salvation brings with it radical changes. *Soteria* and its cognates, then, refer to spiritual and physical healing in the present, leading to final salvation from God's wrath. Paul stresses that justification and reconciliation are in the present, while salvation points to a future event in which God judges the earth and establishes his kingdom. That we await a Saviour was his theme. In summary, we can say that in the NT there is a constant interplay of past, present and future tenses when the word salvation is used: we have been saved, are being saved, and will be saved.

The Perfect Life? Throughout church history scholars have debated whether or not perfection is attainable in this life. Such perfection is defined in terms of the Great Commandment — love of God and man. Guidelines for the perfect life were given by Jesus in the Sermon on the Mount, by Paul in his I Corinthians 13 hymn of love (though he confessed his own imperfection), by the author of Hebrews in the context of persevering under persecution, by John as he elucidated the doctrine of love in his epistles.

The Monastics suggested perfection could be achieved by a renunciation of this world. Wesley saw perfection as part of salvation, hence achievable. Sin for the Christian is willful transgression of known law. Whatever view one takes, this much is clear: "The lives of the saints have always been for Christians the reminder that in this life men and women of all kinds, temperaments and cultures have touched the height of Christian experience and have committed themselves utterly to the service of their fellows. Absolute perfection lies beyond this life, in the vision of God, when faith and hope have passed away, but the love of God endures" (Rupp).

What is that to me? These stages are not discreet entities, nor do they follow a sequential order or time-line: Rather, they are the map of Christian experience. Keep walking. Today's perfection lies in acknowledging I have not arrived. Progress is in stages, first by recognizing a preening self-absorption that alienates people. Confession, asking forgiveness for an act of unkindness, faith in Christ's sacrifice, all lead to redemption, reconciliation with God and with those I offended. I am free. Without realizing it, I move beyond self and enter the world of others where the real battle begins. I offer a hand and pray they will accept it. Though rebuffed, I press on. Those watching show interest and join the pilgrimage.

# THE HOLY SPIRIT

23. The Re-Creator

Yuki cautiously entered the church and took a seat at the back. Everything about the service was old — people in dark kimonos, Bibles covered with embroidered cloth, tattered hymn books, floors varnished the colour of caramel, pulpit overlaid with light and dark brown plywood. Behind it stood pastor Suzuki whose hair blended into the fading black vesture, making the whole seem like one garment from head to toe.

Yet, there were sharp contrasts. From the base of the pulpit dazzling white chrysanthemum pointed upward, overarched by branches woven into a cross. A sharper contrast came when pastor Suzuki spoke:

"Faith makes us new people: cynical teachers become new teachers, old samurai become new samurai. The new samurai is released from bondage to self, in order to serve society. He is not influenced by popularity or antagonism, gain or loss. To the contrary, he is free to pour body, mind and spirit into the task given him. His life is bound up with the lives of others. It finds its meaning there, in sharing their sufferings and joys. This is self-fulfillment, first in the Creator, then in fellow human beings. Such a life becomes a demonstration of what our ultimate goal and direction should be: fellowship, first with the Creator, then with his creatures. Sharing the divine nature infuses us with a quality, an eternal quality, not so much in time but in depth. Our life, then, becomes preparation for that perfect life in heaven with heightened meaning, enduring comradeship, encircling beauty, penetrating joy." Yuki returned the following Sunday, and continued regularly for several months.

In late spring, Yuki and Kazuko surprised the neighbours by performing two sacraments. First, before the Shinto god-shelf Kazuko held a chair while Yuki climbed up with hammer and saw. From the shelf he removed pictures of ancestors, one of which was uncle Ken sitting upright in army uniform, holding a sword in its scabbard. Small cups for food and drink were next. Out came the nails, and Yuki lowered the shelf for Kazuko to hold. They went quietly out in their small garden, Yuki poured kerosene over the shelf and good luck charms, then lit a flame.

Secondly, they walked with pastor Suzuki to the banks of the Chikuma river. Believers held up a cotton sheet for the couple to change into white baptismal garments. Yuki emerged first and walked slowly into the swirling stream. Pastor Suzuki held Yuki's nose and mouth with a white kerchief, then plunged him backward into the water, saying, "I baptize you, Yuki, in the name of the Father, the Son, and the Holy Spirit." Believers were singing now as Yuki walked out dripping and Kazuko waded in, "In the cross, in the cross, Be my glory ever, till my raptured soul shall find rest beyond the river." *(Return to Chaos)*

What is the work of the Holy Spirit? — Throughout history the church has acknowledged: (1) the Holy Spirit as *creator,* not only as the agent of the first creation, but also as the unifying power of the divine that "affects matter from within, so that forms of life can emerge and so that human existence can be spiritual and free" (Rosato). It also means that "there is a spiritual presence in human undertakings, such as art, law-making, ethics, religion and worship," which unites mankind. The Spirit strengthens judges, anoints kings and prophets, to bring about the covenant; (2) the Holy Spirit "as *re-creator* anoints Jesus the Messiah, and mediates his work to the believer. He gives repentance, reveals the Son, illuminates, teaches, empowers, convicts, intercedes, sanctifies; (3) the Holy Spirit as *trans-creator,* working in the church until the consummation of the world. The Spirit empowers the church for world mission."

What does Holy mean? — It is a general term used to signify the distinction between the ordinary and the special, by virtue of an unseen spiritual presence. The OT passage, "you shall be holy, for I am holy" gives God's reason for human aspiration toward holiness. The Jewish people, called out of Egypt to achieve a goal set by God, were taken up with their calling to be a holy people, separate from the peoples around them. In Isaiah, holiness is related to morality, for after seeing the holiness of God, Isaiah was gripped by his own unworthiness.

Jesus addresses God as Holy Father. He prays that his Name should be *hallowed,* that is, made distinct from the creature in the world. Jesus himself is described in the Gospels as the "Holy One," from the circumstances of his miraculous birth, and because, having received the Holy Spirit at baptism, he is bearer of the Spirit. John sees him also as the Holy One of God, who not only bears the same holy nature as God himself but has become in his exalted position the dispenser of the Spirit to men. In Acts he is called the Holy One, looking back to the Holy Servant of Jehovah in Isaiah, anointed by God for the divine mission of saving a lost world. As the Servant of God, Jesus is the holy sacrifice which, itself innocent, is offered vicariously for the guilt of the people of God to open up access to the sanctuary."[1] In the book of Hebrews, Christ is pictured as both priest and victim, entering the Holy of Holies,

---

[1] Otto Procksch, "Hagios," *Theological Dictionary of the New Testament,* Eerdmans, 1964, I. p. 102.

figurative of his entering the abode of God in heaven by virtue of his atoning death, to make effective the New Covenant. From this exalted position he has poured forth his Spirit upon the Christian community to set them apart as a holy community, a temple of flesh and blood, where he can indwell them by means of his Holy Spirit. In Corinthians this temple is termed a living organism. The sacrifice of this church-temple is not an animal victim offered daily, but Christ offered once for all. Paul the missionary ministers in this church-temple, preparing Gentiles for acceptable service to God. Baptism is an external rite but signifies a union with Christ whereby the Holy Spirit as agent renews the moral and spiritual faculties of the believer.

The church or *ekklesia* was comprised of "called out ones." They were called to be a holy nation, a people belonging to God. But they could not realize their holy destiny alone. In Christ holiness is presently realized: "Everything that sustains and redeems the creation as well as everything that cleanses and purifies and fulfills, and everything that empowers faith, hope and love is understood in relation to the holiness manifest in Jesus Christ . . . holiness is hovering over all claims to power, beauty, goodness and truth, confirming and purifying them and pointing them towards God, the Holy One, as their creative ground and final sanction" (Boozer).

24. The Church

What is the Church? On the day of Pentecost, the Holy Spirit as *re-creator* descended upon a group of perplexed believers and formed them into the first *church*. The full meaning of *church* is derived from two Greek words—*kyriake*, which means "belonging to the Lord" and *ekklesia*, meaning "the assembly or called out ones." Hence, "the church is a worshipping assembly called forth by God" (McBrien). The word is used in the singular to denote the universal church, and plural for groups of churches. Various functions and emphases of the church appear in the New Testament: the pastoral epistles (I and II Timothy and Titus) show us a church concerned with "teaching, structure, pastoral care and the survival of the Christian community ... Ephesians and Colossians stress the church as the fullness of Christ, His body, and His spotless bride ...Luke and Acts stress the institutional and charismatic church under the guidance of the Holy Spirit ... John's epistles show an emphasis on the equality of the disciples living in community with the Father and the Son ... James' epistle shows us a church practicing practical piety."

Though there were differences, the following characteristics of the first century church were common: faith in Jesus as the Messiah; practice of baptism and celebration of the eucharist; apostolic preaching and instruction; high regard for communal love; and expectation of the coming of the kingdom of God.

From the time of Augustine there has been a distinction made between the visible and invisible church. The visible church contains a mixture of saints and sinners, whereas the invisible or hidden church consists only of true believers. Luther listed seven marks of the earthly church: the preached Word, baptism, the Lord's supper, administration of discipline, public ministry, prayer and worship. Calvin listed only two: preaching of the Word and administration of the sacraments. Since Vatican II Roman Catholic views of the church have broadened ecumenically to include Anglicans, Greek Orthodox and Protestants.

Who is an Apostle? — The Greek word *apostolos*, from which the word "apostle" is derived, occurs eighty times in the New Testament. In secular nuance it meant *messenger*. "The early church's strong sense of mission, together with a desire to have an appropriate designation for the first leaders of the new movement, caused an obscure Greek word to emerge as a technical term" (Freyne). The term was used of the Twelve sent forth on their mission to Galilee and later confirmed after the resurrection as summing up their mission to the world. For example, Paul uses "apostle" to describe his function of preaching the Gospel, called by God to represent God and Christ in the world, reconciling it to himself. The church today is apostolic in the sense that it continues the ministry of the Twelve and is founded upon them. "Apostolicity, in the sense of faithfulness to the witness of the apostles, is a mark of the whole church," not just its organizational structure.

Who is a Bishop?—The word is derived from the Greek *episkopos*, meaning "overseer." *Episkopos* is used interchangeably with *presbyteros*, meaning "elder." Both terms referred to leaders of the church in Ephesus. And, use of the plural indicates there was more than one official in these communities. By the second century, however, bishop came to be the accepted term for a single chief leader of the Christian community. Ignatius of Antioch (second century) observed and recorded this emerging singular monarchical episcopate. Today "a bishop is the supreme governing, teaching, and liturgical authority in a territory known as a diocese" (Costigan). He has become the "living symbol and principle of unity in the community of faith."

When bishops are in council they are considered successors of the apostles, thus empowered to speak with authority. At first, bishops were chosen by the clergy and people of the area, presided over by the archbishop. Their choices were later confirmed by the pope. At present, bishops are appointed by the pope. Anglicans and some Lutherans still elect bishops.

Who are the Laity? — This word is derived from the Greek *laos,* (people), and is used today to mean parishioners without ordained clerical status. Some scholars maintain that in the NT there is no clear distinction between clergy and laity. All share one common vocation: be people of the new creation. Though Christians have different and complementary gifts and ministries, they hold one common priesthood as the *laos* of God. The word "liturgy", meaning "form of worship," comes from two Greek words — *laos* (people) and *ergos* (work), which joined together reads *people-work.* Worship is the primary function of a believing community, each member participating fully.

In medieval times sharp distinction was made between laity and clergy, but the Reformation brought back a NT emphasis on equality. Lay ministries have developed in modern times: church councillors, local preachers, readers, charismatic prayer leaders, stewardship organizers, etc.

What is meant by Communion of Saints? — It refers to the traditional church belief that living Christians not only have a relationship with each other but with those who predate them. Communion of saints in the NT is based "on their communion with the Father through the Son" (Hanson). But does such communion extend to saints in heaven? The practice of baptizing for the dead in I Cor. "would seem to imply that what we do on earth can affect them," though some interpret "baptizing for the dead" to mean "taking the place of." That is, Paul is not referring to baptismal services conducted after a person's decease, but to present believers being baptized to take the place of fallen comrades. In Rev. the martyrs crying out for judgment "presupposes a knowledge of what is happening on earth." By the third century requests to the saints were inscribed on tombs in the catacombs. By the fourth century, prayers to Mary were officially sanctioned by the Roman church.

What is Confirmation? — It is a ceremony following baptism that developed by 200 A.D., "consisting of a prayer said by the bishop with his hands extended over the candidates, the anointing of the candidates on the forehead, the imposition of the hand on the head of each and the sign of the cross on the forehead" (Whitaker). Yet, because imposition of the hand of the bishop was required, a time-lag developed between baptism and confirmation. Confirmation became reserved for later years in the life of the Christian. Confirmation today is a special service in the church, confirming one's baptismal vows, and qualifying the believer to participate in the eucharist.

What is Consecration? — It is a liturgical act "that asks God to bless, sanctify, and transform that which is set before him" (Fink). Such acts were done in the OT with respect to kings and priests and elders.

"In the NT the transforming action of God is directed to Jesus himself — at baptism, transfiguration and resurrection." The focus is upon God's transforming action on that which is consecrated, whether it be people, bread, wine, or money.

Does Asceticism have a part in church discipline? Asceticism refers to exercises and forms of discipline necessary for a holy life. In Jesus' teachings, however, there are both world-renouncing and world-affirming elements. He taught world-renunciation not out of a dualistic concept of the world as being inherently evil. Rather, it was Jesus' concern for the demands of an uncertain age, asking his followers to renounce certain privileges for the sake of the kingdom. "Traditional Christian ascetical teaching has a good deal to say, which is still relevant, on the necessity for simplicity and austerity in the midst of wealth and plenty. Greater demands are made on inner austerity in modern society, and traditional ascetical teaching is relevant also in the stress it puts on the need for meditation and contemplation" (Tinsley). Greater demands are also put on those embarking on cross-cultural mission. Self-denial is good preparation. "In the words of Bonhoeffer, 'If there is no element of asceticism in our lives, if we give free rein to the desires of the flesh . . . we shall find it hard to train for the service of Christ.'"

How does Repentance differ from Penance? — Repentance is the term used to describe a person's return to God after abandoning a life-style that led away from him. It involves a change in attitude towards God, self, and others, followed by behaviour that reflects that change. But it is essentially oriented toward God. Penance, the Latin form of "repentance," designated "an inner turning to God or a public returning to the church" (Martos), but evolved into a system of penitential acts required by the Catholic church for those seeking forgiveness of sins. "Christians carried out the practice of binding and loosing in the forms of restricting recalcitrant members from full participation in the community, then later releasing them when they mended their ways." Although Jesus enjoined us to forgive the erring, it wasn't until the second century that church leaders began to re-admit apostates publicly. The practice of public penance for grievous sins grew in complexity, sometimes lasting for years, and often done in front of the bishop. During the sixth century Irish missionaries introduced the practice of private confession made to a priest rather than a bishop. Harsh penances gave way to prayers and good works. By the twelfth century the priest's prayer for absolution had turned penance into one of the seven sacraments.

Sixteenth century reformers rejected the idea that God forgives sin through the clergy, asserting that forgiveness is direct from God, needing no intermediary.

25. The Trans-Creator

What does Charismatic mean? — It describes the Christian community when it is "guided by the Holy Spirit, as functioning according to the gifts of the Spirit, including the *charisms* such as prophecy, evangelism, teaching, tongues, healing, and as bonded by the love poured into the hearts of the faithful through the Spirit . . . love gives life to the church; without love the *charisms* have no value" (Faricy). In modern times the word "refers to the movement in the church that emphasizes the renewal of charisms."

Pentecostalism began in the U.S. in 1901. This movement did not have much effect on historic Christian churches until 1960 when it penetrated Reformation, Anglican and Orthodox churches and finally the Roman Catholic church.

What is the Eucharist? — The word comes from the Greek word *eucharistia,* meaning "thanksgiving," and refers to the communion service. "Shortly before his death, Jesus shared the last supper with his disciples, in the course of which he offered praise and thanks to God in the Jewish manner customary on ceremonial occasions" (Martos). It is not clear whether early Christians associated the presence of Christ with the bread and wine elements, but the Bread of Life discourse in John 6 suggests they did. By the second century, the eucharist took on strong tones of being a sacrifice—the action of Christ offering himself to the Father. Around this sacrifice an elaborate liturgy developed, "complete with processions, ecclesiastical vestments and antiphonal chanting." By the middle of the second century a full *agape* meal accompanied the eucharist. Then, "to the brief actions of blessing and sharing were joined prayers, scripture readings, and a homily by the bishop or presbyter."

During the Middle Ages, the eucharist became simplified so that the priest alone in Latin would offer the sacrifice while believers looked on in silence. Aquinas developed the theory that at the time of consecration the substance of wine and bread were transformed into the actual body and blood of Christ, even though the outward appearances were not altered. Aquinas' reasoning went something like this: accidence is the characteristic of an entity that may or may not be, such as a man may be fair-haired (accident) or may not be. But he must be male (essence). The distinction enables the Roman Catholic tradition to hold to *transubstantiation* in the eucharist. This tradition asserts that the *accidents* of bread and wine are not transformed by God's power into the body and blood of Christ, but their inner *essence* is. Such a theory led to a magical view of the eucharist. Only the priest could drink the wine. He must exercise great care to prevent spillage and consume any wine left in the chalice.

Luther's view was slightly different. Called *consubstantiation,* it held that two realities were present in the bread and wine—the foods themselves, and Christ's presence which could be known by faith. The Reformers held two views: (1) the eucharist is merely *commemorative* and symbolic (Zwingli's view, adopted by Baptists and the St. Thomas Evangelical Church of India), or (2) Christ is received *spiritually* during the communion (Calvin's view, adopted by Presbyterians).

The age-old question, "What happens during communion?" is still being asked. New liturgical theologies are emerging. They all attempt to find in the eucharist a relation to "the Last Supper, to Christ's death and resurrection, to the mysteries of incarnation and redemption, to the local Christian community and to the universal church." The Last Supper itself "culminates Christ's ministry of self-giving and anticipates his death for the salvation of others." When Christians today partake of communion, they are "reminded of their calling to live as Jesus did, and they are invited to share their lives and pour out their energies in the service of others."

The Last Supper for Jesus was also a transition from ignominy to glory. As Christians follow his example in sacrificial service, they demonstrate membership in the future kingdom. Because the eucharist recalls great acts of Christ on our behalf, it also calls forth our praise to God for what He has done, a "thanksgiving." Since the Spirit of Jesus indwells the community of believers partaking in the communion, the eucharist not only expresses the unity of the local church of Christ, but is a sign of the oneness of the Church universal, transcending space and time.

Is Christ's death the only focus of worship? No. There are times when focus is on the living Christ. This is called *adoration*, the strongest English equivalent for the Greek word *latreia* which means "to worship." It is an act of obeisance properly reserved for God alone. Preparation for the same homage to Christ is shown in the Gospels by persons bowing and prostrating themselves before Jesus. Worship or adoration of Christ, as demonstrated in the liturgical prayer of Phil. 2.9-11, contributed to the triumph of Nicene orthodoxy in the fourth century. Adoration is not flattery but self-giving love, "made possible by God's first loving us. Like love among humans, our adoration of God expresses itself in gestures, words and silence" (Wainwright).

What is an Icon? The term icon is derived from the Greek word *eikon*, meaning "image." The early church used images in the catacombs and on coffins, but before long a controversy ensued over their use. The *iconoclasts* (anti-image faction) maintained that such usage led to idolatry. In contrast, the *iconodules* (pro-image faction) held that the Christian attitude to material matter is involved in the use of icons or images. They said that man is made according to the icon of God, Christ is the icon of the invisible God, and the Christian is predestined to be formed into the icon of God's son. St. John of Damascus, in defense of icons, maintained that worship of God is forbidden in relation to objects or men *(latreia)*, but veneration of men *(proskynesis)* or objects is not. God himself ordered the making of the cherubim images. Veneration of an image is not to the paint or wood but to that which the icon represents. The *iconoclasts* replied in the Iconoclast Synod of 754 that whoever makes an image of Christ, depicts the Godhead which cannot be depicted. Doing so makes the body of Christ less than divine. According to the *iconodules*, the worshipper who uses icons is reminded of the events of man's salvation, the communion of saints, and the loving economy of God. The icons become windows to the divine through which the worshipper's prayers ascend. The controversy still continues in the church. Though evangelicals point out idolatrous tendencies within liturgical worship, they cannot help but find it difficult to sustain meaningful worship through verbal symbols alone or in unaesthetic facilities.

26. Music

What role does music have in worship? Until postmodernism came East, Indian debate over church music centered on indigenous forms vis-a-vis Western: tabla, drum, or guitar? Indian hymns or English? The issue resolved itself as a matter of *taste*, which unfortunately is a postmodern resolution. It says no music is more conducive to Christian worship than any other. If contemporary musical forms help people worship, abandon traditional ones.

Musicologist Frank Brown enters the contemporary-versus-traditional fray in his book, *Good Taste, Bad Taste and Christian Taste* (Oxford University Press, 2000). "Musical idioms of America's *next church* are contemporary (nothing dating from before 1990 in many cases.) Yet in many of these churches the spectrum of styles offered is actually quite narrow, as it has been in most churches throughout history. Country music is out of the question, as is religious jazz in the style of Duke Ellington (in his *Sacred Concerts*). Nor is there music like that of Sister Marie Keyrouz, a Lebanese nun who has begun singing the chants of her tradition in an appealing secular style that utilizes colourful instrumental accompaniments. The typical *next* music sound is club-style soft rock."[2]

---

[2] Book review in *The Christian Century*, February, 2001, *et passim*.

The author's point is that the *next church* is selective. What is being heard in suburban churches today Brown calls *spiritual minimalism.* If the *next church* wanted to go theologically deeper, its worship teams could find contemporary forms for that, such as songs composed by Ivor Stravinsky or Olivier Messiaen, "all certifiably contemporary and almost shockingly spiritual, and frequently explicitly theological. This would be unremarkable except for the fact that the *next church* and its contemporary Christian relatives claim that theirs is the truly contemporary alternative for Christian music today."

The new generation does not want to be reverent or quiet during worship. Music is the major vehicle for celebration and communication. So what kind of sound track should a church choose? Mega-church musicians find out by asking which radio stations parishioners listen to. *Those that play soft rock* is usually the answer. The church, they say, should use *soft rock* in worship. Classical music and traditional church music in general are relics of the past. If you want life and growth, make use of music, art and media that are culturally relevant.

"Modern church music directors repeatedly emphasize the importance of *quality music,* music produced not by choirs and organs but by praise teams, soloists and a variety of instrumentalists and small ensembles that use synthesizers, drums and electric guitars. Music, especially in the context of youth evangelism, needs to be entertaining.

What about developing a taste for classical music? No, they say. Worship is not the place to teach music appreciation. The only question that worship communities need to ask about music is, *Does it bring people closer to God?* Music is never the message. No form is inherently better than another. Music is good if it makes way for the gospel; it is bad if it doesn't."

Brown warns against churches defining their mission in such terms. Such definition can seriously undervalue the spiritually transformative potential of challenging artistry, both classical and vernacular. Those same values would have had Jesus popularize his image and simplify his message before it was too late.

"What is called for is a studied synthesis of the best of both classical and pop, traditional and contemporary. Bach borrowed from his secular cantatas and harpsicord concerti when composing his sacred works." Martin Luther said he did not want the devil to have all the good tunes. He was openly jealous of the fine music, songs, and precious melodies that Catholics use as masses for the dead, and said 'it would be a pity to let them perish.' John Calvin was extremely cautious about the music he sanctioned for worship: it should exhibit moderation, gravity and majesty.

"It takes informed musical talent to select music addressed to God, not as performance, but as the most intimate and devout communication, a form of speech fit for the ear of the Highest. Gregorian chant serves poorly for lively celebration. By the same token, the latest pop hit serves poorly for meditative prayer. The whole question about inherent meaning and ideology in music eludes a direct answer and is in many ways a matter of intuition that we cannot fully explain.

"Parishioners can distinguish between religious music most appropriate for the inner sanctuary and that which is best for the nave of the church, or for the courtyard, recreational hall or concert stage. They can fittingly choose to use religious music in any one of these settings, but its character and purpose will shift accordingly, with convention playing a role in shaping those choices. But because religious meanings cannot simply be imposed on every sort of musical medium, regardless of its style, considerable musical and liturgical experimentation is required to find out which forms of rock and pop permit or invite stretching for religious purposes. Christians probably need musical laboratories involving both clergy and musicians" (Brown).

With several incisive questions, Brown sums up his argument for discriminating selectivity in adopting secular art forms: "What sort of God are worshippers envisioning as they sing or look or move? To what sort of life and growth do they suppose they are being called? The possibility that a relatively casual and unchallenging style might be all there is to a community's worship life is bound to be deflating to those whose call to discipleship causes them to yearn for something more in aesthetic formation and development . . . this selectivity carelessly done, can inadvertently convert the sacred into something quite ordinary" (Brown).

Shine, Jesus, shine is unquestionably appropriate for a youth rally. But when those same youth appear for worship on Sunday mornings, such words as — *Praise to you, O God Almighty, You are Lord eternally, All creation lauds your glory* — set to Beethoven's Ode to Joy, are also unquestionably appropriate.

27. Worship

What is the Liturgical Movement? — The liturgical movement is regarded as having begun in the Roman Catholic church at the Benedictine Abbey of Solesmes in the late nineteenth century. A parallel movement took place in the Church of England during the same period under the Tractarians. This movement stressed three aspects of Christian faith: "True understanding of the incarnation, producing a deeper appreciation of the dignity of human life. True understanding of the sacrifice of Christ, producing a commitment to sacrificial living. True understanding of the church as the body of Christ, creating a deeper sense of community both in life and in worship" (Jasper).

The task of liturgical theology is to make clear the meaning of worship. It stresses that belief and doctrine begin and end in worship and prayer. The classical liturgies are a primary source for thought about God, creation, redemption, etc. Liturgical theologians interpret the meaning of the eucharist, baptism and confirmation rites, daily prayer, pattern of readings and prayer over cycles of the seasons. They focus on such concepts as "remembering, invocation, thanksgiving, blessing and praise, offering and sacrifice" (Saliers).

What is the Church Calendar? Time is the theater of divine activity. We honour this gift from God by careful planning and diligence. The three cycles of the church calendar are *annual, weekly, and daily.* Each cycle turns on the same event—Jesus' resurrection which occurred at Passover (yearly), first day of the week (weekly), and early in the morning (daily) (light out of darkness). Thus, the Christian calendar punctuates natural time *(chronos)* with an event that is above time—the resurrection, and also looks forward to an event in time—Christ's return. Like a ship sailing over the sea, the church moves between these two points—the resurrection and the return. The early church observed these cycles as follows: (1) daily, by scripture reading and prayer, (2) weekly, by scripture reading, preaching and the eucharist, (3) annually, by baptism and confirmation preceded by Lent (40 days).

To these main cycles others have been added: to the daily reading and prayer has come the eucharist; to the weekly Lord's Day has been added fasting (Friday in Roman Catholic tradition); to the annual cycle has been added *Epiphany* which celebrates the baptism of the Lord; *Christmas,* celebrating Jesus' nativity; *Advent,* lasting four weeks in preparation for Christmas or Epiphany; and *Holy Week* preceding Easter, days that focus on the triumphal entry, the institution of the supper, and the crucifixion" (Allen).

28. Ministry

What is Christian Ministry? — "Christian ministry is a ministry of salvation in the service of the world. All baptized are called to share in this service in accord with their states of life, special gifts and roles within the social structure of stable Christian communities. All forms of ministry have three basic traits: (1) proclamation of the gospel of Jesus Christ, (2) service of the needs of the neighbour, and (3) worship of God" (Kilmartin). Such ministry should lead to response in faith by those who hear God's word, to recognition of the person's worth before God as that person is served by the church, and finally to a communion with God and with each other.

There has been a divergence of interpretation regarding the role of those ordained to the ministry — bishops, elders and deacons. One extreme stresses the dependence of the community upon the few ordained, giving them a *paternalistic* role. The other stresses mutual dependence of all upon one another, giving the ordained ministry a *partnership* role. It would appear from I Cor. 12 that Paul avoided both extremes of paternalism and partnership. Rather, there seems to be a NT emphasis on "the common life in Christ through the mutual sharing of the gifts possessed by each member." Thus, those ordained neither monopolize gifts and responsibilities nor do they merely preserve order among independently functioning groups within the church. Through the rite of ordination the "community expresses and acknowledges that the candidate is called by God for a special service." Consequently, the community affirms that it is God who ultimately calls, commissions and empowers ministers to foster the life and unity of the community as a whole.

What is the Kingdom of God? — The expression is freely used in the NT and refers primarily to the rule of God in the hearts of men. "The kingly rule of God is certainly present in the person of the King-Messiah; but it will be fully manifested only at the end of time" (Sharpe). The tension throughout church history has been between present and future aspects of the kingdom. "The early church expected the final manifestation of the kingdom in the very near future. But as this original hope waned, the kingdom came to be identified either with the visible church itself, or with the rule of Christ over the individual believer."

Luther considered the kingdom of God synonymous with the realm of divine grace, while Calvin saw the kingdom embodied in a theocratic society, "where individuals might play an active part under God." Evangelicals have linked the extension of the kingdom with missionary work, while liberal theologians have identified the kingdom with ideal social conditions on earth. "This latter view opened the way for a secularization of the kingdom idea in terms of notions of progress, development, evolution, and material prosperity." However, the disillusionment of world wars in the 20th century has given more credence to the view that the kingdom will not be realized until Christ comes again. From the mid-1960s there has come a renewed interest in the kingdom as an ideal society "characterized by equality, justice and truth . . . conservatives still tend to regard the kingdom in its individual and future aspects, liberals in its corporate and present aspects."

Is there such a thing as Christendom? — The word means the *Christian world*. In a narrower, political sense, it only applied to that period of the Middle Ages when the church could enforce obedience to its discipline in belief and practice. The height of its power was in the eleventh century when the pope humbled the emperor at Canossa.

Christendom disintegrated with the rise of nationalism, the Reformation, and the Renaissance. We use the word today in an apolitical sense to refer to the church worldwide regardless of denomination.

Index

A

Adoption 105
Adoration of Christ 130
Aesthetics 13
Analogy 9, 19, 39
Anonymous Christians 26
Anselm 53
Anthropology 85
Anthropomorphism 35
Apocrypha 35, 36
Apologetics 14
Apostle 46
Apostles Creed 5, 46
Approaches to theology 4, 27
Aquinas 8, 24, 33, 50, 104, 128
Arianism 70, 79
Asceticism 125
Atheism 48, 54
Atonement 74-75
Augustine 47, 88, 121
Autonomy 90-92
Avatara 69-70
Awareness 23

B

Barth 9, 15, 25, 97

Balthasar 80
Beauty 13
Biblical theology 27
Bishop 122
Brahmanism 9, 48, 93
Buddhism 25, 56

C

Calling 99
Calvin 47, 74, 88, 89, 103
Canon 36
Carey 25, 109
Catechism 36
Character 107
Chardin 80
Charismatic 127
Chinese symbol system 10
Christendom 141
Christian ministry 138
Christology 78
Church 120
Church building 13
Church calendar 137
Communion 10
Communion of saints 17, 123
Confirmation 124

Confucianism 50
Conscience 21, 99
Consubstantiation 129
Consecration 124
Conversion 100
Cosmological argument 51
Cosmology 57
Creation 56, 92
Creator 9, 47, 48
Critical realism 19
Cross 71
Culture 86

D

Darwinism 92
De Nobili 24
Dharma 31
Dialectics 15
Docetists 79
Dogmatic theology 30

E

Enlightenment 92-93
Epistemology 16
Eucharist 127
Evil 94
Existence 53

F

Faith 100, 108

G

Gospel 37
Grace 62

H

Heber 25
Hegel 95
Hermeneutics 38
Heteronomy 90
Hidden Christians 15
Higher criticism 8, 92
Hinduism 25, 32, 48, 56
History 18
Holy 117
Holy Spirit 117
Human language 8, 17
Hume 95

I

Icon 130
Idolatry 46
Ignatius 122
Imitation of Christ 70
Incarnation 69
Indigenous theology 31
Islam 7, 24, 55

J

Jainism 48
Jerome 36
Justification 104
Justin Martyr 79

K

Kant 16, 49
Karma 18, 31, 64
Kerygma 38
Kingdom of God 37, 121, 139
Kraemer 25

L

Laity 123
Lewis, C. S. 12, 17, 96
Liturgical movement 136
Logos 5, 14, 24, 39, 85
Lull, Raymond 24
Luther 24, 47, 71, 103, 106, 129

M

Ministry 138
Miracles 61
Moral argument 52
Moral theology 30, 32
Music 132

N

Names for God 50
Natural theology 8, 29
Nestorian 7
NT theology 27-28
Niebuhr, Richard 88
Nirvana 31

O

OT theology 29
Ontological argument 53
Open view of God 34
Otto, Rudolph 9

P

Parable 39
Paradox 15
Pentecostalism 127
Perfection 95, 110
Perseverance 105
Philosophy 19
Plotinus 47
Polytheism 48, 55
Postmodernism 5, 92
Prayer 59
Preparatory truth 26
Process theology 33
Providence 58

R

Rahner, Karl 26
Ramabai, Pandita 71
Re-Creator 117, 120
Redemption 73
Religious experience 21, 29
Repentance and penance 125
Resurrection 75
Revelation 7
Ricci, Matteo 24

Index

S

Sadhu Sundar Singh 32
Salvation 110
Samsara 18, 31
Sanskrit 9, 25, 64
Schleiermacher 49
Science 19
Sense data 16
Shintoism 50
Statues 13
Strong, Augustus 50
Symbol system 10

T

Tabula rasa 24
Teleological argument 51
Teresa, Mother 58, 71, 73
Theology of the Cross 71
Theonomy 90
Tillich, Paul 5, 38, 47, 50, 53
Tolstoy 88
Trans-Creator 117, 127
Transubstantiation 128
Typology and Allegory 40

U

Unknowability of God 17

V

Vedanta Monism 93

W

Water buffalo theology 32
Witness 108
Worship 131

X

Xavier, Francis 24

Z

Zoroastrianism 96
Zwingli 129

Milton Keynes UK
Ingram Content Group UK Ltd.
UKHW030851111124
451035UK00001B/160